TARIFF AND SCIENCE POLICIES
APPLICATIONS OF A MODEL OF NATIONALISM

D.J. Daly and S. Globerman

Tariff and Science Policies:
applications of a
model of nationalism

PUBLISHED FOR THE ONTARIO ECONOMIC COUNCIL BY
UNIVERSITY OF TORONTO PRESS
TORONTO AND BUFFALO

© Ontario Economic Council 1976
Reprinted 2015
ISBN 978-0-8020-3338-3 (paper)

Library of Congress Cataloging in Publication Data

Daly, D.J.
　Tariff and science policies.

　(Ontario Economic Council research studies; 4)
　Bibliography p.
　1. Tariff – Canada.　2. Science and state – Canada.　3.
Nationalism – Canada.　I. Globerman, S., 1945-　　joint
author.　II. Title.　III. Series: Ontario Economic
Council. Ontario Economic Council research studies;　4.
HF1766.D25　　　382.7'0971　　　76-24911
ISBN 978-0-8020-3338-3 (pbk.)

This study reflects the views of the authors and not necessarily those of
the Ontario Economic Council.

Contents

Tables

Preface

A fairly extensive dialogue is continuing to take place in Canada on the goals, meaning, and merits of economic and cultural nationalism in Canada. The term nationalism is broad enough to encompass a wide range of interpretations, policy instruments, and diverse groups of supporters. One important source for ongoing debate has been the neglect of a systematic framework to assess the effects of nationalism.

However, some economic models have been developed which provide a potential framework within which the costs can be evaluated and the potential benefits and beneficiaries identified. Harry Johnson has developed a theoretical model of nationalism which provides important insights into the sources and nature of economic nationalism and offers certain testable hypotheses. The most important conclusions suggested are that nationalistic policies will raise prices to consumers and lower real incomes of urban workers below their potential levels. On the other hand, the major beneficiaries of nationalistic policies would be the managers and more highly educated members of the labour force.

This study does not attempt a complete assessment of nationalism. Its aim is to test the implications of the model of nationalism with the available evidence in two important policy areas: commercial policy and science policy in Canada. One of the authors has previously studied the differences in performance between Canadian and US manufacturing and the role of tariffs in those differences, and also the differences in backgrounds of management in the two countries. The other author has previously studied the differences in the speed of diffusion of new processes in Canada and other countries, and some aspects of research and development in Canada. The study draws on available statistical data and related earlier work, but is integrated to test the proposed model in these two areas of application. It draws interrelations between tariffs and the diffusion of technology, and has implications for the competitive position of Canadian secondary manufacturing. The study explores the related policy implications.

The authors gratefully acknowledge comments on an earlier draft from Peter Cornell, Harry Johnson, Abe Rotstein, Ronald Wonnacott, and a number of anonymous referees from the Ontario Economic Council which financed the study.

D.J.D.
S.G.

TARIFF AND SCIENCE POLICIES
APPLICATIONS OF A MODEL OF NATIONALISM

1
Summary and conclusions

This initial chapter recapitulates some of the main conclusions of the complete study and provides some perspective by highlighting important points. The policy implications are also indicated as well as suggestions for further research.

The theoretical framework developed in Chapter 2 draws heavily on the economic theory of nationalism of Albert Breton and Harry Johnson, and the aim of the monograph is to apply that framework to two policy areas in Canada – tariffs and science policy. Quantitative data are used wherever possible, using the United States as a basis of comparison. This theoretical analysis suggests that nationalistic policies would raise prices to consumers, and lower real incomes of urban workers below potential. On the other hand, the beneficiaries of the tariff would be the managers and more highly educated members of the labour force.

Chapter 3 looks at the costs of tariffs, emphasizing the aspects applicable to the model of nationalism. A series of studies has established that Canadian prices of manufactured products are more expensive to the consumer and more costly at the manufacturing level than prices of comparable items in the United States. Although there are differences in rates of indirect taxes and in trade margins, the tariff and related pricing policies of manufacturers are critical in the higher levels of prices to consumers. The incidence of these taxes is relatively higher on low income receivers.

Tariffs also have an important depressing influence on the levels of productivity in Canadian manufacturing. This is associated with plant sizes which are less than optimum scale in a larger market, and with a wider range of products being produced in a Canadian plant of a given size than in the comparable industry in the United States. In 1963, the level of output per person employed in total manufacturing was more than 30 per cent lower than in the United States, with considerable variation from one industry to another. Very little narrowing had occurred in the following decade for total manufacturing.

This evidence on the lower levels of performance in Canadian manufacturing is consistent with the estimate of the costs of the Canadian and United States tariffs, made by Ronald and Paul Wonnacott, of 10.5 per cent of Canadian GNP in 1963, and with the revised estimate made by Ronald Wonnacott for 1974. These estimates for Canada are larger than those for other countries, partly because an accurate assessment has been made of costs in the form of less efficient production methods as well as in costs to the consumer.

The evidence on lower levels of real national income and manufacturing output per person employed has been well established by earlier studies. The new area explored in this monograph concerns the effects of tariffs on the distribution of national income – a key part of the model of nationalism.

These influences of tariffs were reflected in lower average weekly earnings in Canadian manufacturing than in the United States, after allowing for slight differences in the consumer purchasing power in the two countries. From about 1952 to 1966, the gap was approximately 20 per cent lower, but this had narrowed to about 4 per cent in 1974. The gap has narrowed relatively more in Ontario than in Quebec, but Ontario is still about 13 per cent below the key large adjacent manufacturing states in the Northeast. The increases which have occurred in output per man-hour in Canadian manufacturing have been only slightly greater than in the United States since 1963. As a result, the narrowing in output per person employed has been less than in money and real earnings. The costs of the tariff thus clearly fall on the consumer and the urban worker, as suggested by Johnson's analysis.

A potential beneficiary of the tariff would be the scarce factor of production, and the evidence surveyed suggests that trained managerial manpower is the scarce factor of production in Canada, based on supplies of the main productive factors relative to the United States. The managerial group in manufacturing is about 2 per cent of the total labour force, and manufacturing accounts for about one-fourth. Evidence indicates that Canadian managers have a lower level of formal education than their United States counterparts, fewer have degrees in business, and more have entered middle and senior levels of management much later in their working lives. The benefits to this group lie more in the number of managerial positions and the lesser degree of competitive pressure than in higher incomes relative to other groups within Canada.

The discussion of the tariff and the emphasis on productivity have important implications for the regional distribution of tariffs and the effects of lower

tariffs or free trade. The consumer costs are felt in all regions, but tariff reductions would lead to a further narrowing in real wage and productivity differences between Ontario and Quebec and adjacent regions in the United States.
Within 400 miles of the manufacturing belt from Windsor to Quebec, there are
twenty states containing more than 100 million people with a total non-farm
personal income six times the comparable Canadian income. This region is a
major source of materials and components and is a major market outlet within a
reasonable overnight truck drive of Ontario manufacturing. The continuance of
Canadian tariffs would permit high domestic costs in manufacturing to persist
and would make Canada a high-cost source of supply even if United States tariffs
were eliminated.

Turning to science policy, the main statements of goals in science policy and
the related legislation are consistent with the nationalist model. Specifically,
existing and proposed policies emphasize the creation of more job opportunities
for Canadian scientific and technical workers. Particular encouragement is given
to the indigenous development of new technology of a 'break-through' nature,
rather than to the rapid diffusion of existing new products and techniques that
could have a quicker and more predictable impact on output and performance.

Studies of the diffusion of three new production processes showed a consistent pattern of slower adoption rates in Canada than in the United States or in
Europe for one process related to paper manufacturing. Average plant size and
product variation within plants were found to be significant factors influencing
Canadian adoption patterns for the various innovations. The major supplementary empirical findings of the diffusion studies indicate that limitations on
realized scale and specialization – largely attributable to the domestic
tariff – impose certain long-run costs upon the domestic economy by reducing
rates of technological change. In effect, higher costs to consumers and lower
factor payments associated with tariff-induced production inefficiencies reflect
an interaction between the failure to exploit 'static' scale economies, the per-
petuated use of capital equipment that does not embody 'best practice'
technology, and slower adoption of new products and processes than in other
countries.

These results have important implications for policy. One conclusion is
that important benefits could accrue to Canadian consumers and urban
workers from further reductions in tariffs and non-tariff barriers to trade in
Canada and elsewhere. The real wage differences between Ontario, Quebec, and
adjacent manufacturing states have narrowed appreciably, especially since 1966,
but there is still scope for additional narrowing, and reductions in trade barriers
are an important route for further increases in real income.

It is also important that other policy measures be taken to facilitate the
adjustment from the current high cost, low productivity position in secondary

manufacturing to a more competitive position in international markets. Measures to facilitate that adjustment would be an adequate level of domestic demand, slower reduction in Canadian than foreign tariffs, and measures to increase the supply of trained managers.

Current science policies emphasize the encouragement of research and development in support of innovation. However, only a small proportion of new projects and processes reach the production stage, even in large markets. In a small market, the main beneficiaries of research and development aimed at producing significant technical advances are likely to be the scientists in the jobs thereby created. Moreover, in the absence of empirical information, an implicit assumption has existed that failure to innovate is the source of a Canada-United States technology gap and that economic and cultural proximity to the United States ensures rapid adoption in Canada of products and processes developed in the United States. Much of the recently emerging evidence belies this notion and suggests that achieving increased efficiency and greater international competitiveness in Canadian industry requires that higher priority be given to encouraging more rapid *diffusion* of new technology. Openness to change and higher levels of managerial and entrepreneurial skills are – among other factors – central to achieving this goal.

In a country with a small population and labour force, it is not really possible to keep up to date in all areas of manufacturing. Instead of spreading limited supplies of managerial and scientific skills over all areas, it may be preferable to concentrate resources on a more limited range of products and industries in which Canada has a comparative advantage. These products have a better chance of penetrating the export markets and spreading the overhead costs of research and development and the start-up costs of new products, processes, and facilities over long runs than over short runs associated with the small domestic market.

FUTURE RESEARCH

This monograph has tried to answer certain questions, but it has also led to some new questions being asked. One useful research topic arising from this study is the need to be more specific on Canada's areas of comparative advantage – both current and prospective. Without a more systematic and deliberate assessment of areas of strength and weakness in both factor supplies (human resources, non-renewable natural resources, and renewable physical capital assets) and relative efficiencies in relation to world markets, there is no realistic basis for assessing possible alternative industrial structures and the associated level of real national income. Such an assessment could be useful both for private decisions under a pattern of freer trade and for public discussion of an industrial strategy, which can otherwise remain vague with no criteria of purpose.

This study has assessed tariffs and science policy and how these nationalistic policies can affect potential national income. However, other studies have questioned the desirability of the goal of economic growth and raised questions about the associated costs (of pollution, urban growth, etc.). There have also been studies that suggest the economic growth experienced in the past is on the verge of being checked and reversed by limits to growth – the supply of non-renewable natural resources, the supply of food, the problems of pollution. How great are these costs of economic growth, and are these possible checks to growth imminent or exaggerated? A reassessment of the goal of economic growth in the light of a restatement of old questions and concern about some new ones would be useful.

Chapter 3 emphasizes the key role of management in either initiating or resisting change. Significant changes in tariffs and non-tariff barriers in Canada and other countries would have important implications for Canadian management. This monograph develops the rationale for potential benefits of national-istic policies accruing to management. Although our analysis suggests that this is plausible, data on hours worked and income are inadequate for a rigorous test. More data and analysis would be desirable.

The economic analysis of the distributional effects of tariffs on prices and incomes poses questions about the decision-making process in Canadian com-mercial policy. Could the relatively small managerial group have such an in-fluence on policy making that the real costs can continue to fall on the much more numerous consumers and urban workers in manufacturing and other industries? The interconnections between elites and new work by sociologists and political scientists may be of value in a renewed look at the domestic political process in commercial policy.

2
Introduction and analytical framework

There has been a significant increase in the extent of economic integration in the world economy in recent decades. This tendency has been accelerated by a general reduction in tariff barriers – through a series of multilateral tariff negotiations and the formation of a number of important regional common markets or free trade areas. A further round, currently being negotiated, will also re-examine non-tariff barriers. Economic integration has been facilitated by relatively lower transportation costs (checked by the increases in oil prices and airline fares since 1973); a further important element has been the growth of the multinational corporation.

At the same time, economic and cultural nationalism has persisted in many countries, both industrialized and developing, perhaps with an even greater degree of public discussion. It is interesting that the increased economic integration has not necessarily led to integration along political and cultural lines (Lyon, 1975; Black, 1974).

Ramsay Cook has suggested that Canadian nationalists have concerned themselves with three primary questions: national unity (including French/English relations and federal/provincial powers); relations with Great Britain and, to a lesser extent, with France; and relations with the United States (Cook, 1971, 201). The political independence of Canada from the United Kingdom is long established. In addition, the reduced economic strength and slow economic growth of the United Kingdom have resulted in a reduced share of Canadian exports going to that country. Consequently, the primary emphasis on the international side has been concentrated on the United States.

The current concerns of those who would class themselves as Canadian nationalists are many, and the lists of concerns of different self-styled nationalists may not be identical. On the economic side, these concerns might include the extent of foreign ownership and control; the degree of research and development in Canada; the extent of exports to the United States; the heavy dependence on exports of natural resource products (including the extent of processing before export); the limited degree of exports of manufactured products; the extent of interest and dividends paid abroad; the presence of non-Canadians represented in senior management and on boards of directors of subsidiaries in Canada; the purchase of Canadian companies, real estate, and recreational land by foreigners. In the areas of culture and communication, there is also a range of concerns including such topics as Canadian content and advertising in radio and television, periodicals, and publishing as well as faculty and material in universities.

It is not the purpose of this study to describe, assess, or interpret this broad spectrum of shifting areas of interest and concern. It should also be noted that self-styled nationalists cover a wide range of political views from right-wing bankers and businessmen to left-wing groups such as the former Waffle wing of the New Democratic Party. There need be no unanimity among them on such policies as tariffs. A number of authors and studies, both governmental and private, have explored some aspects of nationalism in Canada from the economic, cultural, and political points of view (Fayerweather, 1973; Gordon, 1966; Levitt, 1970; Murray and LeDuc, 1975; Rotstein 1973; Rotstein and Lax, 1974; Watkins, 1968; Wahn, 1970; Gray, 1975).

This study has a narrower objective with basically a threefold purpose:
1 to outline a theoretical framework to assess the economic aspects of nationalism in Canada;
2 to assess the actual or potential costs of tariffs in two policy areas – commercial policy and science policy (especially innovation and diffusion) – and the subsequent effects on real incomes in Canada, in the perspective of real income differences between Canada and the United States;
3 to analyse and identify the effects of nationalism in these two policy areas on prices and the distribution of incomes, with special emphasis on those groups within Canada who would be protected or encouraged by nationalistic economic policies.

Both policy areas (commercial policy and science policy) are important and controversial, and are particularly significant for the provinces of Ontario and Quebec because of their heavy concentration of manufacturing. As a result, this study gives some, but not exhaustive, consideration to the regional implications.

THE THEORETICAL FRAMEWORK

The primary sources for the theoretical framework for the present work are earlier studies by two Canadian economists, Albert Breton and Harry Johnson. Breton initially developed the framework in considering nationalism in the province of Quebec, and Johnson's fullest discussion of the theoretical framework is in the context of new and developing states. To our knowledge, neither of these nor any previous study has applied the framework systematically and quantitatively to Canada in any published form. The following summary of their concepts is put in more general terms as a basis for testing their conclusions in the two selected policy fields for Canada, emphasizing elements that will be examined more fully in later chapters. The major aim of this study, however, is to test the reasonableness of the existing theory rather than to develop a new one.

Breton's article was published in 1964 and was applied to the developing aspects of Quebec nationalism and the provincial nationalization of eleven private power companies (Breton, 1964; 1972). Political nationalism encourages changes in the distribution of property and ownership of wealth, and encourages a modified flow of monetary and non-monetary rewards.

The most important component of the monetary flow of rewards accrues in the form of high-income jobs which ownership makes available for members of a given national or ethnic group. If we distinguish between middle-class and working-class jobs, the occupations made available for a given group of nationals are mostly middle-class occupations ... Because of this, some people will be paid more than they are worth because they are of the 'proper' national origin and/or more people will be employed than is economically optimal (Breton, 1964, 377-8).

Harry Johnson uses the 1964 article as a basis for his later study.

Using this framework, Breton produces a number of specific and testable propositions about nationalism: a nationalist policy is mainly concerned with redistributing income rather than with increasing it; specifically, the redistribution is from the working class to the middle class; consequently, where the working class is poor, there will be a tendency to resort to confiscation rather than the purchase of property. Furthermore, nationalism will tend to favor investment in national manufacturing, since manufacturing jobs and ownership are preferred by the middle class; its collective nature will appeal to socialists; and its emergence will be correlated with the rise of new middle classes who have difficulty in finding suitable career opportunities (Johnson, 1967, 4).

In summarizing the article, Johnson draws three major implications from this theory of nationalist economic policy.

One implication is that nationalism will tend to direct economic development policy along certain specific lines; these lines might represent economic optimality, and would do so if the conditions posited by some familiar economic arguments were present. Failing empirical validation of these arguments, however, the consequence will be a reduction of material production below the economy's potential. In the first place, nationalist economic policy will tend to foster activities selected for their symbolic value in terms of concepts of national identity and the economic content of nationhood; in particular, emphasis will be placed on manufacturing; and, within manufacturing, on certain industries possessing special value symbolic of industrial competence (such as the steel and automotive industries). Second, nationalist economic policy will foster activities offering prestigious jobs for the middle class and/or the educated class; the nature of such activities varies with the stage of development: very undeveloped countries favoring bureaucratic jobs offering steady incomes for routine work; more advanced countries favoring managerial and professional jobs suitable for the products of the educational system; fairly mature countries favoring jobs in higher education and research.

Another implication is that nationalism will tend to direct economic policy toward the production of psychic income in the form of nationalistic satisfaction at the expense of material income.

If attention is confined to material income alone, a third implication is that nationalism will tend to redistribute material income from the lower class toward the middle class, and particularly toward the educated middle class; in this respect, nationalism reinforces the trend of modern society toward the establishment of a class structure based on educational attainment (Johnson, 1967, 13-14).

This framework for the analysis of economic nationalism tends to be descriptive and is based on much reading, first-hand experience, and discussion of these issues in many countries. Although the presentation relies heavily on deductive reasoning, it needs amplification for practical testing. The key questions, it seems to us, are empirical. The four main questions raised by Johnson's model, which will be considered in Chapter 3 on the costs of tariffs to Canadians as an illustration of the model of nationalism, are as follows:

1 What are the costs of tariffs in terms of potential real national income in Canada?

2 What are the results in terms of prices of manufactured products to consumers?

3 What are the effects in terms of real wages in Canadian manufacturing and levels of output per person employed?

4 Are the beneficiaries of the tariff the managerial group in Canada (as suggested by Johnson), and what is the nature of such benefits?

The study will try to be as quantitative as possible, and will give special attention to the position of Ontario and Quebec — the key manufacturing belt in Canada.

It might be noted that recognition of the desirability for empirical research on economic nationalism is not new. In a review of *The Canadian Quandary*, Mel Watkins expressed sympathy with the general nature of Johnson's argument, but felt that

... his logic may have limited appeal to many potential readers, and particularly businessmen — whose influence on economic policy is so important — of pragmatic bent and limited forensic skills ... The moral of these ... points seems to be that more empirical work is necessary on the nature and causes of Canadian economic nationalism in the hope that we can exorcise this devil from our midst, without, hopefully, increasing our susceptibility to worse varieties (Watkins, 1972, 373).[1]

Thus far, the discussion of the economic theory of nationalism has emphasized a static framework at a point in time. The costs to the consumer and the urban worker are based on the prices and real wages in adjacent regions in the United States. However, policies of economic nationalism can also influence the dynamic aspects of technological change and the speed of diffusion of new products and new processes through the economy. The increased interest in economic growth has been reflected in more theoretical and applied work in industrial organization and international trade. (Posner, 1961; Hufbauer, 1966; Hirsch, 1956; Vernon, 1966; Gruber, Mehta, and Vernon, 1967; Wells, 1972; Vernon, 1970; Wilkinson, 1968, 113-25, 138-9; Baumann, 1974.) Chapters 4 and 5 of this study use some of these concepts and tools to analyse empirical evidence on the speed of diffusion of new processes and products in Canada compared with other countries; how tariffs can influence the overall rate of technological change in Canada compared with other countries; and how tariffs can influence the extent and nature of research and development expenditures.

Before turning to the application of the Breton-Johnson model to the two specific policy areas, it might be helpful to the reader to outline the new elements in the following analysis.

---

1 The review was initially published in the July 1964 issue, but Watkins has subsequently revised his views.

1 We believe this to be the first attempt to apply the Breton-Johnson model of economic nationalism to *any* country. The effects of commercial policy and science policy (two important areas) on the distribution of income, both to Canada and to Ontario, will be explored.

2 Although studies have been done on tariffs and commercial policy in Canada (including the recent report of the Economic Council of Canada and the supporting staff studies), Chapter 3 contains a quite comprehensive and current discussion of wages, productivity, and costs related to Canadian manufacturing in the context of commercial policy.

3 This is the first serious attempt to look at management as a factor of production in any country and the conditions under which it could benefit from protectionist policies, and to examine the evidence (admittedly imperfect) on differences in management backgrounds in Canada and the United States.

4 Most recent studies of science policy in Canada have emphasized research and development; this study emphasizes diffusion of technology. It includes new evidence, and a fresh and documented interpretation of the slow diffusion of technology in Canada.

5 This is the *first* Canadian study dealing with the interrelationships between tariffs, on the one hand, and research and development and diffusion of technology, on the other. The analysis emphasizes the role of tariffs in explaining current Canadian practice in domestic manufacturing at a time when much recent Canadian material has excessively emphasized foreign ownership and control.

6 Both commercial policy and science policy have a very direct bearing on manufacturing, which is heavily concentrated in Ontario and Quebec. Later chapters include some discussion of the regional implications of these policies.

Although the above points emphasize new elements of analysis, this study also draws on earlier work in these two fields—witness the extensive references and bibliography at the end of the study. Without this earlier work by others, it would have been impossible to keep the current study to manageable proportions and to bring it to completion.

In areas as important and controversial as these, however, the attempt to introduce new elements of interpretation, when the existing data are imperfect and reflect a variety of factors operating simultaneously (either reinforcing or offsetting in direction), is bound to lead to controversy, as has been reflected in the responses from readers of a first draft. It is to be hoped that this study can be followed by others with more and later data, and that the model will be applied to other aspects of economic nationalism. The authors make suggestions for further research, some of which grew out of comments by earlier readers.

3
The costs of tariffs

In this chapter, a key one in the study, the available evidence on the costs and beneficiaries of tariffs in Canada is explored. A number of separate and distinguishable, but interrelated, considerations are involved and it seems desirable to set down briefly the order in which they will be considered. Initially, the current importance and relevance of tariffs and commercial policy for Canada will be outlined, followed by some discussion of the role of economic considerations in policy. One of the traditional costs of tariffs is the welfare loss to consumers from higher prices of manufactured products, apart from the income transfer to the government from tariff collections. A further cost that can be distinguished is on the production side. Tariffs can lead to lower levels of output per person employed and lower real incomes to those employed in manufacturing by encouraging home production to replace imports. This effect has been given limited, but increasing, recognition in the literature, but the evidence on and discussion of this topic have probably gone further in Canada than in any other country. The next section identifies the major beneficiaries of the tariff, testing the hypotheses suggested previously by Harry Johnson. The regional effects of the tariff are then considered, with special attention being given to the role of Ontario and the probable implications for real incomes, markets, and industrial location. The final section explores some related policy considerations related to a change in commercial policy strategy, such as a high level of employment, adjustment policy, competition policy, and tax and monetary policy coordination.

THE CURRENT IMPORTANCE OF COMMERCIAL POLICY IN CANADA

Commercial policy has played an important role in government for a century. The tariff of 1874 produced a relatively simple tariff structure – primary products entered free, while partly processed goods paid 5 to 10 per cent, and most finished manufactured goods paid 17½ per cent. The changes made in 1879 by Conservative Finance Minister Tilley introduced a much more elaborate schedule with substantial increases in rates and a number of specific duties. Canadian tariff rates reached their maximum level early in the 1930s but reductions were made in 1935 and 1938. Since World War II, Canada has participated in the series of multilateral tariff reductions, so that the current levels of rates are well below the peak levels reached in the early part of the 1930s. Tariffs and their regional and industrial effects have been a continuing area of economic and political discussion in this country and two serious attempts at tariff reciprocity with the United States (in 1854 and 1911) were considered but not implemented (Mackintosh, 1940; McDiarmid, 1946; Barber, 1955; Young, 1957; Eastman and Stykolt, 1967; Wonnacott and Wonnacott, 1967; Dales, 1966; Wonnacott and Wonnacott, 1968; English, Wilkinson, and Eastman, 1972; Economic Council of Canada, 1975, 95-9). At the present time, however, a number of factors justify a new look at this topic, which has been under recurrent review, change, and reassessment for the last century in Canada.

For one thing, major regional free trade arrangements (such as the European Common Market) have been implemented concurrently with multilateral tariff negotiations. This has been particularly important in Europe, where the European Common Market is currently being enlarged to form a market for the industrial products of 250 million people. Other national markets are also large – the United States with more than 200 million people, and Japan with more than 100 million. This leaves Canada, with a population of about 22 million as almost the only industrialized country in the western world without access to a large, free-trade market. (Daly, 1973; Geiger, 1973, 6-17; Economic Council of Canada, 1975, 95-9). Size of markets for manufactured products is an important factor in productivity and costs, and this topic will be developed further later in this chapter.

Second, a new round of multilateral tariff discussions is under way, and Canadian options and policies are being reassessed as part of that series of discussions and negotiations. The priority of these discussions in the United States and the European Common Market countries, and the positions the major countries take, will be critical to the success of the negotiations, but the results for Canadians can be significantly affected either by taking a more outward-looking stance to achieve a more competitive position in manufacturing, or by following a more cautious and defensive posture as was taken in the Kennedy Round of negotiations of 1964-67.

Third, the increased degree of economic nationalism has overtones for such goals as economic growth and the efficient use of resources within Canada. Some authors have been encouraging more nationalistic policies, sometimes as part of a broader industrial strategy, but often they fail to consider the effects on the size and distribution of the national income, or whether the policies are in line with Canada's comparative advantage. Some orders of magnitude of the costs and benefits of policies could facilitate a more objective assessment of the issues.

The three considerations outlined above suggest that a reassessment of Canada's commercial policy and options is desirable. At the same time, a number of conceptual and statistical developments have been accumulating that permit a more quantitative and specific assessment of commercial policy on the size and distribution of the Canadian national income. We shall draw on the key results of this work to assess the applicability of the Breton-Johnson model to Canada's commercial policy. This newer work reflects the framework of economic growth pioneered by Edward F. Denison and applied to real income differences between Canada and the United States; the emphasis on the production effects of the tariff on productivity and real earnings in manufacturing; and the emphasis on effective (in addition to nominal) tariff rates.

Although this study concentrates on tariffs, it is recognized that important non-tariff barriers exist and that these have tended to become relatively more important in Canada and other countries as tariffs have been reduced. Some of these non-tariff barriers affect manufactured products (such as the limits on low-cost imports from Japan and other Asian countries), while others relate to agricultural products, or preferences on government purchasing and construction contracts. The general topic of non-tariff barriers is excluded to keep the present study within manageable limits. Tariffs are a much more important source of protection for manufacturing, which is the primary concern of this monograph, than for mining and agriculture, which receive relatively more protection from tax concessions and subsidies respectively. In 1970, nominal tariffs provided about 9.6 per cent of the protection out of a total of 12.4 per cent for tariff and non-tariff protection combined (Economic Council of Canada, 1975, 17; Grey, 1973; Stegemann, 1974; Pestieau and Henry, 1972).

ECONOMIC CRITERIA FOR POLICY

Many considerations and points of view can be brought to bear on a topic as large and controversial as economic nationalism. The training and skills of an economist can be used to suggest orders of magnitude of the costs of a policy, and to identify the beneficiaries, using the earlier Breton-Johnson framework as a basis of the analysis.

As a criterion for assessing the effects, this study will emphasize the implications of the policy alternatives on real national income per person employed and per capita.[1] This is consistent with some of the goals set out initially by the Economic Council of Canada in their *First Economic Review* (restated in later Reviews), and draws on the conceptual framework for economic growth developed by Ed Denison (Denison, 1962; Denison and Poullier, 1967; Denison, 1974; Walters, 1968, 1970; Daly and Walters, 1967; Daly, 1972*a, b*).

The study will also look at the *distributional* effects of the policies being considered; for example, the effects of the presence of tariffs on consumers, on workers in manufacturing in both Ontario and Canada, and on the beneficiaries. By assessing the economic costs and the beneficiaries, the general public and the government will be in a better position to assess the options and the alternatives, and to consider whether the benefits of any non-economic goals and objectives are still worth the costs.

---

1 Two points in this criterion should be emphasized. One is that real national income, apart from price differences, will be used. This should be widely accepted as appropriate in light of the magnitude of the rate of price change in Canada, as well as in many other countries in the world, during the mid-1970s. The second is the emphasis on a per-person basis rather than on total national income. A per-person basis is a more appropriate measure for welfare purposes. Furthermore, the rate of growth in population and of the labour force in the Canadian economy has been more rapid than in any other industrialized country during the 1960s and 1970s, and this should be allowed for. Also, the proportion of the total population in the Canadian labour force historically has been much below that in other countries, and this is expected to continue, although the difference has been diminishing for more than a decade.

It is also recognized that the existing national income measures were designed to facilitate the analysis of changes in demand on a short-term basis, and some rearrangements and modifications are desirable either to analyse longer-term supply factors, or to emphasize consumer welfare. These modifications have been used where appropriate in some of the published studies that will be drawn on where applicable.

It is clear as well that some writers have emphasized the costs of economic growth and minimized the benefits (e.g., E.J. Mishan, *The Costs of Economic Growth* [Harmondsworth, England: Penguin Books Ltd., 1969]). Later studies for the United States by Nordhous and Tobin suggest that alternative measures of economic growth and welfare that allow for some of the other costs and benefits of economic growth not normally included in national income do not radically alter the conclusion that significant increases in real levels of consumption and living standards have been occurring. These questions will not be explored further in this study. See also Andrew Weintraub, Eli Schartz, and J. Richard Aronson, eds., *The Economic Growth Controversy* (White Plains, N.Y.: International Arts and Sciences Press, Inc., 1973); and Wilfred Beckerman, *In Defence of Economic Growth* (London: J. Cape, 1974).

THE COSTS TO THE CONSUMER

It is widely recognized that the consumer in Canada usually pays higher prices for manufactured products in Canada than are paid for comparable products in the United States. This was a major theme of the study done by John Young for the Gordon Commission (Young, 1957, 63-73, 161-233). A subsequent study by the Dominion Bureau of Statistics for May 1965 found that, on the average, prices of manufactured products at the consumer level were about 10 per cent higher than in the United States (Prices Division, 1967).[2] The higher costs of manufactured products at the consumer level may not only reflect differences in costs at the manufacturer's level associated with the tariff, but could also arise from differences in the manufacturer's sales tax, which is relatively more important in Canada than indirect taxes in the United States, differences in wholesale and retail margins, and differences in transport costs.

Earlier studies and analyses have indicated that the tariff is the *key* factor in the higher level of prices at the manufacturer's level, before taxes have been added. For example, John Young's study of the cash cost of the Canadian tariff was designed to compare manufacturer's prices in Canada *ex tax* and the price of an identical good laid down at the same point by a foreign supplier *ex customs duty*. Young concluded that these cash costs to the consumer amounted to between 4½ and 5½ per cent of GNP in 1954. He also pointed out that these estimates could be on the low side, as manufacturing production was temporarily depressed in that year by the mild business cycle recession of 1953-54, and did not include any allowance for government purchases at the higher price level (Young, 1957, 70.) Although the Young study includes price relatives (ex tax) for individual items and product groups, an overall difference in prices of manufactured products does not seem to have been calculated. In comparison with a level of Gross Domestic Product in manufacturing in 1954 of $6,785 million, however, the costs of the tariff in that study would be reflected in prices about 10 per cent higher.[3]

2 Price data from the worksheets of the consumer price indexes were initially matched with the prices of comparable items in the files of the United States Bureau of Labor Statistics. Special pricing for some additional commodity specifications, which were included in the Canadian consumer price index but not in the comparable American specifications, was also done by DBS staff in selected American cities.
3 The cash costs of the Canadian tariff in 1954 were estimated at $610-$753 million, compared to Gross Domestic Product at Factor Cost in Manufacturing of $6,785 million in 1954. Ibid., p. 72, and unpublished estimates from the National Accounts Division of Statistics Canada.

All later studies of manufactured goods prices have essentially confirmed the main conclusions from Young's study relating to 1954, indicating higher prices and costs at the plant level. A.E. Safarian obtained results from 173 company returns to a mail questionnaire sent out late in 1960. About two-thirds of the companies and two-thirds of the reporting industries indicated unit costs as being higher in Canada (Safarian, 1966, 201-17). A series of company interviews and a subsequent mail return on costs per unit were obtained for a staff study for the Economic Council of Canada. Of thirty-one identical manufactured items produced in both countries, eighteen had total costs *20 per cent or more* higher than the same item in the United States and eight cost 35 per cent or even more to produce in Canada. Although the number of commodities represented was small, the companies regarded them as fairly representative of their total output (Daly, Keys, and Spence, 1969, 12, 96-7). This study concentrated on secondary manufacturing and was not designed to cover all manufacturing. The price difference for total manufacturing would not be that large.

A much more comprehensive statistical study was done subsequently by Craig West, using census of manufacturing data for Canada and the United States. Using United States quantity weights, prices in Canada for total manufacturing were 10.9 per cent higher than in the United States. This is roughly comparable to the relative price difference for manufacturing in 1954 obtained from John Young's study for the Gordon Commission. However, if allowance is made for the differentials in input costs between the two countries and other adjustments, the value added costs were about 25 per cent higher in Canada in 1963 (West, 1971, 26). This reflects the tendency for costs in non-manufacturing to be more like those in the United States than costs in manufacturing. There is considerable variation around that total for the twenty-nine individual manufacturing industries which could be analysed separately. On a net value-added price basis, prices in Canadian sawmills were 56 per cent of the American level, while those for wool yarn were 223 per cent. Only ten industries had lower prices in Canada, while nineteen were higher (West, 1971, 18-22). This diversity for individual industries within manufacturing around the total points up the importance of having a comprehensive estimate of the price difference. This same pattern of diversity around the mean in value-added relative prices will also appear in the diversity in output-per-worker relatives. It is probable that both these tendencies are related to the greater dispersion around the average in effective tariff rates than nominal tariff rates.

It is widely recognized and accepted that the key factor in the higher prices for manufactured goods in Canada than in the United States is the presence of the Canadian tariff. Canadian manufacturers tend to regard the American domestic price, plus tariffs and transportation costs (with any adjustment for the

TABLE 1

Effective average tax rates per family unit, 1969
federal import duties, Canada and Ontario

Family money income class ($)	Canada	Ontario
Under 2,000	0.072	0.081
2,000- 2,999	0.033	0.029
3,000- 3,999	0.023	0.024
4,000- 4,999	0.019	0.018
5,000- 5,999	0.019	0.017
6,000- 6,999	0.016	0.016
7,000- 7,999	0.016	0.015
8,000- 8,999	0.015	0.014
9,000- 9,999	0.014	0.014
10,000-10,999	0.013	0.014
11,000-11,999	0.013	0.012
12,000-14,999	0.012	0.012
15,000 and over	0.009	0.009
All Classes	0.014	0.013

SOURCE: Allan M. Maslove, *The Pattern of Taxation in
Canada* (Ottawa: Information Canada for the Economic
Council of Canada, 1973), pp. 94, 95, 100, and 101

exchange rate if appropriate), as an upper limit on the prices they can charge in
Canada. However, there is also some evidence to suggest that the companies will
frequently operate with prices somewhat below this upper limit.[4]

In the context of the Johnson model, it is of interest that the incidence of
federal import duties tends to fall relatively more heavily on low income groups
both for Canada as a whole and for Ontario (see Table 1). This reflects the
tendency of low income groups to spend heavily on commodities in relation to
their income.

Estimates of the cash costs of the tariff have been made for many other
countries. The general approach is similar in other countries, but the estimates
are rarely made with the same degree of detail as in the Young study for
Canada. Furthermore, the estimates of the costs or the gains from a customs
union or free trade are usually much less, sometimes amounting to only a few
tenths of one per cent of GNP (Janssen, 1961; Harberger, 1959; Johnson, 1958;

4 Examples of primary steel, fine paper, automobiles, and price changes after devaluation
early in the 1960s are mentioned in Daly, Keys, and Spence, *Scale and Specialization*,
pp. 32-3.

Leibenstein, 1966; Scitovsky, 1958; Wernelsfelder, 1960). The estimate for Canada of 4½ to 5½ per cent of GNP in 1954 may partly reflect the relatively greater importance of the imports of manufactured products to GNP in Canada than in some of the other countries studied.

The estimates by Young, and those for most other countries referred to in the above paragraph, assume constant costs and similar production conditions with and without a tariff. These estimates are often based on assumed import demand elasticities and may, therefore, miss important cost components. Since these assumptions exclude the production costs of the tariff, they are biased downwards, an aspect that will be considered in the following section.

PRODUCTION EFFECTS

Most estimates of the costs of tariffs are limited to their costs to the consumer. Typically, these estimates assume similar production conditions in the country for which they are being made as in the rest of the world, and constant returns to scale.[5] They also usually allow only for the tariffs in the country concerned, and do *not* allow for the effects of tariffs and non-tariff barriers in *other* countries on the exports of manufactured products and the national income of the country being estimated.

Recent work on the Canadian tariff has extended the concept of the costs of tariffs from the usual conceptually restricted limit of the costs to the consumer (summarized in the last section) in two directions. The study by Ronald and Paul Wonnacott (1967) broke new ground conceptually by extending the costs of the tariff to include the production effects, which involved abandoning the

5 The gain from free trade (or the cost of the tariff) is based on the concept of consumers' surplus, introduced by Alfred Marshall, which would measure the triangle under a demand curve for a single product, and allow for the difference in price and quanfity purchased, with and without a tariff. The estimates would be affected by the tariff rate, the price elasticity of demand in the relevant range, and the relative importance of that product in consumption and national income. The estimate excludes the tariff revenue to the government. To allow for the concerns of modern welfare economies, the demand curve should reflect a compensated demand curve, which could involve some compensation within the country between losers and gainers. For a fuller discussion of the concepts, see such references as Harry G. Johnson, 'The Cost of Protection and the Scientific Tariff,' *JPE*, August 1960, 327-45, reprinted in Johnson, *Aspects of the Theory of Tariffs* (Cambridge: Harvard University Press, 1972), pp. 187-218; and Ronald J. Wonnacott and Paul Wonnacott, *Free Trade Between the United States and Canada: The Potential Economic Effects* (Cambridge: Harvard University Press, 1967), pp. 270-304. It should be noted that the Johnson (1960) article did *not* allow for the effect of the tariff on techniques of production while the Wonnacott-Wonnacott (1967) study did.

inappropriate assumptions of constant returns to scale and similar production conditions in different industrialized countries, and to include the effects of United States tariffs on Canada (Wonnacott and Wonnacott, 1967; Wonnacott and Wonnacott, 1968). Additional studies have examined the extent to which plants in Canada were less than optimum size for their process or product, and had a greater degree of product diversity and short runs associated with tariffs (Eastman and Stykolt, 1967; Fullerton and Hampson, 1957; Daly, Keys, and Spencer, 1968). This section will recapitulate that evidence, including data and discussion of developments since the early 1960s when some of the studies were completed, dealing initially with the major effects at the plant, company, and industry levels and, subsequently, the total costs of tariffs to Canada.

The presence of the Canadian tariff leads to higher prices for manufactured products in Canada (both to the consumer and at the factory level), and makes it possible to introduce plants of less than optimum size, sometimes to serve local markets.[6] The industries covered in the Wonnacotts' volume include fruit and vegetable canning, cement, containerboard, shipping containers, synthetic detergents, major electrical appliances, newsprint, meat packing, petroleum refining, primary steel, and rubber tires. It should also be noted that engineering-cost studies for a number of continuous flow industrial products indicate lower costs with larger size plants, especially in the petroleum and chemical fields (Haldi and Whitcomb, 1967). For a number of the basic chemical salts, the production of a large modern plant is greater than the demand of the whole Canadian market, which has been served in the past by several smaller plants.

A recent study by Scherer reaches similar conclusions on the tendency for plant sizes in the twelve industries studied for Canada to be suboptimal in size. For twelve industries studied, both the mean and the median of the individual indices were about half the size of American plants. (Scherer, 1973, 135). Estimates of the minimum optimum production scales were prepared by company interviews on the basis of engineering estimates, assuming 1965 'best practice' technology. In some industries, these minimum optimum scales were

6 The Eastman-Stykolt volume emphasizes plant size, using the statistical data on optimum plant size developed by Bain, using primarily American data. Bain has subsequently applied this framework to a number of countries, including Canada. See Joe S. Bain, *International Differences in Industrial Structure: Eight Nations in the 1950's* (New Haven: Yale University Press, 1966). Both studies emphasize the high proportion of plants in individual Canadian industries that are less than optimum size, based primarily on American experience. However, neither study gives serious consideration to the differences in length of run and degree of specialization for plants of the same size in comparable industries in the two countries, which is emphasized in the next part of this study.

TABLE 2

Canada: Top 50 per cent plant sizes as a percentage of the minimum
optimal scales, and cost penalties with suboptimal scale operation

Industry	Top 50 per cent plant sizes as % of minimum optimal scales	Percentage by which unit cost rises building at 1/3 minimum optimal scale
Beer brewing	26	5.0
Cigarettes	31	2.2
Fabrics	187	7.6
Paints	32	4.4
Petroleum	38	4.8
Shoes	110	1.5
Bottles	118	11.0
Cement	83	26.0
Steel	92	11.0
Bearings	97	8.0
Refrigerators	13	6.5
Batteries	63	4.6
Mean value	74	n.a.
Median value	73	5-6.5

SOURCE: F.M. Scherer, 'The Determinants of Industrial Plant Sizes in Six
Nations,' *The Review of Economics and Statistics*, May 1973, Tables 2 and
3, pp. 137 and 138

changed over time, frequently upward. Data were also obtained on the extent to
which unit costs increased if plants were one-third the minimum optimum scale.
These data are included in Table 2. It is of interest that in the industries where
costs increase the most at one-third optimal scale (glass bottles, Portland cement,
and integrated steel), half the Canadian plans were close to that minimum
optimal scale. Cement and iron and steel are two of the industries in Table 3
which have higher levels of net output per employee in Canada than in the
United States. In only three industries were a majority of Canadian plants close
to, or under, one-third of the minimal optimal scale (brewing, cigarettes, and
refrigerators). For two of these industries (cigarettes and refrigerators), the levels
of net output per employee in 1963 were well below the American level. An
important piece of new information is that for about half the industries covered,
costs are only 5 or 6 per cent higher, even when a plant is only one-third the
minimum optimal scale (Scherer, 1973, 137-8). These results suggest that the
differences in plant size can only explain a small part of the differences in costs
per unit between the two countries.

A further widespread phenomenon, which has been emphasized by Canadian industrialists, is the prevalence of short runs. In a number of Canadian industries the range of items produced in a typical plant is usually substantially larger than in a plant of the same size in the United States (Fullerton and Hampson, 1957, 61-93, 147-62; Knox, Barber, and Slater, 1955, 43-52; Eastman and Stykolt, 1967; Daly, Keys, and Spence, 1968, 20-5; Wilkinson, 1968, 109-13). This was reflected in higher costs per unit of output and lower levels of output in relation to capital and labour input than in comparable industries in the United States. Company officials could give examples of dramatic increases in output if the American length of run could be achieved – both a steel company official and a fine-paper official provided evidence that output would triple with the same labour and capital under those circumstances (Daly, Keys, and Spence, 1968, 43-4).

However, their analysis suggested that there was no incentive for an individual company to try to specialize on its own initiative. Officials in Canada were usually familiar in detail with current practices in the United States whether their companies were wholly owned in Canada or subsidiaries. Thus, lack of knowledge was not a factor and no engineering or technical procedures prevented the use of the techniques in Canada. (A fuller treatment of the diffusion of technology will be provided in Chapter 5.) Although one company could achieve a big increase in productivity and reduce internal costs per unit, value added in each company was frequently only a small part of total costs because of the importance of purchases from other firms and industries that would continue unchanged. Only small reductions in total cost could be achieved in spite of spectacular increases in output per person employed within an individual firm. On the other hand, significant reductions in price would be necessary to sell the additional output. If the demand were relatively inelastic in the range of the prevailing price, total revenue and total profit to the company would actually be reduced! Under these circumstances, greater profits could be obtained at lower levels of productivity than with potentially higher levels (Daly, Keys, and Spence, 1968, 43-6).

This emphasis on specialization and length of run reflects the incorporation of modern cost theory into the analysis. Since Alfred Marshall, classical cost theory has emphasized the role of plant size in costs, developing this notion for a single product plant. However, even for single product plants, there are data to indicate lower real costs with greater experience of workers and managers, and lower costs per unit when a large number of items have been produced than with a small number of items. The theoretical rationale and illustrative examples of the applicability of these notions have been developed by Alchian and Hirshleifer (Alchian, 1959; Hirshleifer, 1962, 235-55).

In a recent paper, based on extensive interviews and studies of costs in twelve industries for six countries, F.M. Scherer stated that such product-specific scale economies are more significant to costs 'in the sense that of a doubling of individual production run lengths from average 1970 levels would lead to a greater percentage reduction in costs than a doubling of average plant sizes, all else equal' (Scherer, 1974).

The preceding pages have summarized the effects of tariffs on the decisions made by business firms within Canada (irrespective of the nationality of the owners and managers) with respect to plant size and product diversity. Although a significant number of business firms have been covered in interviews, and the main conclusions have been drawn on, it is also useful to summarize the main statistical results to provide orders of magnitude for individual industries and total manufacturing.

The differences in real net output per employee in Canadian manufacturing and a number of key individual industries are shown in Table 3 for the year 1963. For that year, the level of total manufacturing for Canada was 68.5 per cent of the United States level, or about one-third lower on a per employee basis. There is, however, considerable diversity from one industry to another, so that a number of industries have higher levels of real net output per employee in Canada (e.g., sawmills, cement manufacturers, hosiery mills, iron and steel, etc.), while most industries have lower levels, with the gaps being quite dramatic in certain cases (e.g., wool yarn mills, feed manufacturers, tobacco products, slaughtering and meat packing, etc.). Although one might expect some correlation between the tariff rate and the magnitude of the productivity difference, statistical tests of this hypothesis have been negative (West, 1971, 55-6[7]).[8]

The presence and size of tariff rates have a clearer and more significant impact on Canadian exports and imports than has thus far been found in the

---

7 Nominal tariff rates were used, but the coefficient was small and not significant at the 10 per cent level. When export industries were excluded, the coefficient for the nominal tariff remained small and not significant. A grouping of some of the industries covered by West into high and low tariff and high and low concentration industries was not consistent with the hypothesis that the productivity gap would be wider for high tariff industries. The concentration classification uses the one developed by Harry Bloch in 'Prices, costs, and profits in Canadian manufacturing: the influence of tariffs and concentration.' In *Canadian Journal of Economics* 7, 594-610.

8 The selection of industries for detailed study emphasized those with a high degree of homogeneity of output to facilitate the collection of appropriate data for output and intermediate inputs. However, the most striking examples of product diversity occur in the non-sampled industries, and this is reflected in a wider productivity gap for total manufacturing than in the sample industries. This limits the opportunity for any possible effects of an association between higher tariffs and a wider productivity gap to be reflected in statistical tests of significance for the individual industries covered in the West study. The small sample size, the use of nominal rather than effective tariff rates, or the omission of other possibly relevant variables may also be contributing factors to the absence of the expected results.

TABLE 3

Real net output per employee by manufacturing industry in 1963
(Canadian output ÷ U.S. output, in per cent)

Sawmills	151.5	Motor vehicles and parts	72.0
Cement manufacturers	125.2	Men's clothing	67.3
Hosiery mills	109.6	Soap and cleaning supplies	64.6
Iron and steel	103.0	Dairy products	63.4
Veneer and plywood	102.8	Confectionery	60.4
Ready-mix concrete	101.5	Other paper converters	60.0
Bakeries	94.3	Concrete products	55.6
Pulp and paper	93.6	Paints and varnishes	54.4
Poultry processing	89.9	Battery manufacturers	53.7
Fabricated structural	86.3	Petroleum refineries	44.9
Rubber industries	85.0	Slaughtering and meat packing	38.8
Sugar refineries	82.2	Tobacco products	36.5
Shoe factories	79.7	Feed manufacturers	33.1
Soft drinks	79.2	Wool yarn mills	9.2
Alcoholic beverages	76.3		
Total for all manufacturing industries (after adjustments for comparability)	68.5		

SOURCE: E.C. West, *Canada-United States Price and Productivity Differences in Manufacturing Industries, 1963*, Staff Study No. 32 for the Economic Council of Canada (Ottawa: Information Canada, 1971). United States price weights are used in combining the individual components.

productivity differences. The merchandise trade data are consistent with the view that tariffs tend to reduce both exports and imports. In multiple regressions of Canadian imports, Bruce Wilkinson found Canadian nominal tariff rates were an important depressing factor in secondary manufacturing imports, and the result was statistically significant in most equations. He also found that exports of Canadian secondary manufacturing products were reduced to a statistically significant degree by Canadian nominal tariff rates; the level of effective tariff rates in the United States also had a negative, but not statistically significant effect. However, he pointed out that it would have been preferable to use Canadian effective tariff rates, and also that the presence of both positive and negative correlations in the 'independent variables' introduced the possibility of multicollinearity (Wilkinson, 1968, 144-51).

A recent study by Baumann found that high effective Canadian tariff rates depressed the share of Canadian imports to domestic production to a significant extent, and that the American effective tariff rate depressed the share of

TABLE 4

Output per person employed – Canadian and U.S. manufacturing
selected years (U.S., 1963 = 100)

Year	Canada	U.S.	Canada Below U.S. (%)
1953	45.6	76.4	− 40.3
1963	68.5	100.0	− 31.5
1973	100.5	142.7	− 29.6

SOURCE: Table 1, extended by Statistics Canada, *Aggregate
Productivity Measures, 1946-1972* (Ottawa: Information Canada,
1974), p. 58; *Statistics Canada Daily*, April 7, 1975; and unpublished worksheets kindly made available by the same agency

Canadian exports to domestic production to a statistically significant extent.
The net balance of trade is affected by the level of both American and Canadian
effective tariff rates, but the Canadian rates are relatively more important
(Baumann, 1974*b*).

It is of interest to extend the results for Table 3 on the gap in levels of real
net output per employee in total manufacturing to earlier and later years. This is
particularly important in light of the narrowing in average weekly earnings in
manufacturing between Canada and the United States since the latter part of the
1960s. In 1963, the Canadian level was 31.5 per cent below the United States,
and was still about 30 per cent below the American level in 1973. The differences for selected individual years are shown in Table 4.

One can only speculate on the reasons for the modest narrowing that has
taken place. One possible factor is the reduction in tariff rates implemented
during this period. A second possible factor is the increased specialization that
has taken place in the automotive and automotive parts industries in Canada – a
topic that will be considered in the context of the estimates of the costs of
tariffs to Canada. A further possible explanatory factor is that a major part of
the fresh capital and technological resources of the United States has been
consumed by the military in the last twenty-five years. After 1965, the rates of
productivity increase in the United States dropped sharply relative to previous
experience and the performance of other countries (Melman, 1975).

Estimates of the costs of the Canadian and United States tariffs on manufactured products to Canada have been made by Ronald and Paul Wonnacott
(1967) and Wonnacott and Wonnacott (1968). They concluded that 'the total
cost of both North American tariffs to Canada is estimated as approximately
10.5 per cent of Canadian GNP ,' with the estimates relating to 1963 (Wonnacott

and Wonnacott, 1967, 299; Wonnacott, 1975, 177).[9] They drew on the Young estimate of the cost to the consumer, and made their own estimate of the production costs on the basis of the share of manufacturing wages in Canadian GNP, the percentage difference in money wages in 1963, and the exchange rate difference in the same year. The depressing effects of the North American tariffs on Canadian wages were estimated to be equivalent to 6.06 per cent (Wonnacott and Wonnacott, 1967, 298). These orders of magnitude are in general agreement with the estimates of the productivity difference in manufacturing made by West for 1963, and the company interviews done for the *Scale and Specialization* study in 1966 and 1967. These estimates include an allowance for the effects of United States tariffs on Canadian manufacturing. The rationale for this is that Canadian production would be so small relative to American production that it would not affect the American price; Canadian firms would be price takers in the American market and would have to absorb the American tariff. Prices to the Canadian firm would thus be lower by the extent of the United States tariff on any exports there (Eastman and Stykolt, 1967, 22-5; Daly, 1972*a*).[10] This tariff would also block out potential Canadian exports, thus further accentuating short runs and high costs.

It is of interest to note the implications of free trade on federal government revenues. The estimate of the cost of tariffs to Canada amounted to about $5.3 billion in 1963, which excludes import collections to the federal government as these are internal transfers. In that year, customs import collections were $577 million, slightly more than one-tenth of the cost of the tariffs! By discouraging imports, customs revenue can vary inversely with the costs of protection. At the 1963 federal tax rates (excluding the tariff), the additional federal revenues from the higher level of Canadian GNP would more than offset the loss in customs revenues. When additional revenues at the provincial and municipal levels are

9 The only other direct estimate of the cost of the two tariffs to Canada is by Williams, but this estimate is based on the assumption of unchanged input-output coefficients and does not allow for economies of scale with free trade. His estimate of 4 per cent is unrealistically low. See James R. Williams, 'The Canadian-U.S. tariff and Canadian industry.' Mimeo. (Hamilton: Department of Economics, McMaster University, 1973).

10 Roma Dauphin has suggested that the American tariffs fall on the American consumer rather than the potential Canadian exporting firm. However, the American studies on which he relies probably have in mind low-cost suppliers for the products affected, and for such situations the American tariff presumably would fall on the consumer. However, Canadian manufacturers of secondary products are typically high-cost producers, are price takers, and this argument would not apply to Canada. Roma Dauphin and Gerald Audet, 'The regional impact of freer trade in Canada,' a background study for the Economic Council of Canada. Mimeo. (Ottawa: Economic Council of Canada, 1974).

allowed for, the increase in total government revenue is even greater. This illustrates the scope for potentially higher government revenue from a larger economy to be used for tax reduction, reduced budget deficits, or new functions of government to be undertaken without increasing tax rates. The revised estimate of the benefits from free trade for Canada for 1974 suggest that comparable gains in other government revenues to offset lower customs collections would still be applicable.

A number of commercial policy developments have taken place since 1963 which would contribute to lower estimates of the static costs of tariffs if the identical concept were to be re-estimated in 1975. For example, the Canada-United States Automotive Agreement has led to a drastic reduction in the number of models produced in Canada and to a significant reduction in the wage and productivity gaps between the automotive and automotive parts industries in the two countries (Beigie, 1970, 1972). In addition, the reductions in the tariff rates made by both the United States and Canada during the Kennedy Round negotiations have been implemented, and some effects on greater specialization have already occurred (Lermer, 1973; Baumann, 1974a).

In addition, a significant narrowing in money and real wages has occurred since 1963. (This development will be discussed more fully in the next section.) Further, the exchange value of the Canadian dollar has appreciated. The exchange rate and the difference in money wages were critical components in the estimate of the production costs of Canadian and American tariffs in the estimate for 1963.

As part of a study of Canadian trading options, Professor Wonnacott has recently updated the earlier estimate. The revised and improved estimate gives a slightly smaller estimate in relation to GNP than the earlier one, as illustrated by Table 5. The earlier estimate for 1963 had been made by the individual items in the right-hand column. Subsequent studies and data permitted the making of a new, more current estimate of the components on the left side of the table, which emphasizes the key sources of the increased real incomes to Canadians from free trade with the United States. The recent discussion recognizes that the mid-1970 position could involve a disequilibrium in money wages in manufacturing and/or the exchange rate in light of the modest narrowing that had taken place in the Canada-United States productivity gap in manufacturing.

This revised estimate of the gains to Canada from free trade with the United States of 8.2 per cent for 1974 is slightly less than the 10.5 per cent estimate for 1963 published in the 1967 volume. This reflects the gains that have already accrued from the rationalization of the auto industry following the Auto Agreement and the reductions made following the Kennedy Round. However, the Wonnacott 1975 study recognizes that this estimate may be conservative as it

TABLE 5

Estimation of benefits for Canada of a free trade area with the United States, 1974

Sources of Benefit (real terms)	Per cent of GNP	Realization of these benefits	Per cent of GNP
A Comparative advantage specialization	} 2.3	I Price reduction	4.0
B Recapture of duty revenue on Canadian exports previously paid to U.S. Treasury		II Increase in equilibrium wage	4.2 (residual estimate)
C Increased productivity of labour and other factors of production in Canada because of economies of scale	5.9	III Increase in equilibrium returns to other factors	
Total benefit, as generated:	8.2	Total benefit, as realized:	8.2

SOURCE: R.J. Wonnacott, *Canada's Trade Options*, Study for the Economic Council of Canada (Ottawa: Information Canada, 1975), p. 177

does not allow for changes in the pattern of consumption, does not allow for increased returns to the non-labour factors of production, and is based on increased productivity in manufacturing only in Canada and not for other industrial sectors (Wonnacott, 1975, 179, 181, 182). Furthermore, these gains relate only to the gains from a free trade area with the United States and not the most desirable policy alternative on economic grounds, multilateral free trade.

However, these estimates are the static costs of the two tariffs to Canada. Additional dynamic considerations could arise from higher savings and capital formation associated with a higher, rather than a lower, level of GNP (Wonnacott, 1975, 20-22). This effect is not likely to be large in the Denison framework for economic growth, in light of the relatively low share of income attributable to non-residential structures and equipment, about 15 per cent in Canada in the 1950-62 period (Walters, 1970, 58-9). A potentially more important factor could be the dynamic aspects of greater output in relation to total factor input – the more rapid adoption of new technology, more aggressive, younger, and better-trained management, and a greater degree of competition within the Canadian market. These areas will be discussed more fully later in this study.

TARIFFS AND THE DISTRIBUTION OF INCOME[11]

The evidence in the two earlier sections has pointed up that the costs of tariffs are relatively large in relation to GNP, measured both in terms of costs to the consumer in the form of higher prices and costs in terms of lower levels of real output in relation to labour and other factors of production being used in manufacturing. These conclusions are relatively well supported by economic theory, quantitative data for total manufacturing and individual industries within manufacturing, and company interviews. The current section moves into an area that is more complex, more controversial, and one that has apparently not been previously explored for Canada or any other country.

Four areas that contribute to the difficulty of fully clarifying and resolving the interrelated issues involved will be considered:

1 The presence of Canadian tariff and non-tariff barriers simultaneously with the presence of tariff and non-tariff barriers in other countries on manufactured products, whose effects on money incomes in Canada can be in opposite directions;
2 the desirability of introducing management explicitly into the analysis as a necessary factor of production;
3 differences in the effects of tariffs on the distribution of income in the short and long run;
4 the facts on the distribution of income and the degree to which tariffs may have been a contributing factor in any Canada-United States difference.

These four areas will be explored in turn, and in each case the nature of the reasoning and the evidence in relation to testing the applicability of the Breton-Johnson model will be considered.

1 Domestic and foreign trade barriers

The earlier sections of this monograph have emphasized the effects of the Canadian tariff on prices of manufactured products and the differences in productivity (through less than optimum plant sizes and short lengths of run) relative to the United States. However, Canadian manufactured products would also encounter tariffs in other countries when and if costs in Canada began to approach those in potential markets. This section will sketch briefly the analysis applicable to this situation, and return to the topic again in subsections (3) and (4) below.

It is generally recognized that the short-term effects of the introduction of a tariff on manufactured products would be to raise the prices of those products

11 This section has benefited from extensive comments and questions by a number of external reviewers and positive encouragement and suggestions from Harry Johnson.

by roughly the extent of the tariff, and prices would continue to persist above world prices because of the tariff. Until existing and new firms can adjust plant sizes and introduce new products, these higher prices will be reflected in higher incomes to the factors of production (both labour and capital). However, in the longer term, when new firms enter, new plants are established, new product lines established domestically, and so on, it is unlikely that the rates of return to capital or the real earnings of workers in manufacturing could persist at higher levels. This is especially improbable if many of the effects of domestic tariffs are reflected in lower levels of output per worker both in manufacturing and in the economy as a whole. However, if barriers to entry or monopolistic elements persist, higher factor prices could persist.

On the other hand, if Canadian manufacturers are looked at as price takers in the United States market (the largest, closest, and more comparable world market), the presence of tariffs in that market would reduce the prices received by potential exporters by the extent of the American tariff. In the short term, incomes of Canadian factors of production would be *depressed* by the introduction of a tariff in other countries. This is the *opposite* direction to the impact effect of Canadian tariffs.[12]

This creates a difficult problem in assessing the available evidence later, since the available data on income differences in the two countries will reflect the net effect of two opposing forces. In practice, however, the American tariff has little short-term relevance for prices and incomes in the secondary manufacturing area, as the Canadian tariff puts manufactured goods prices *above* American prices and effectively limits Canadian production to the domestic market.

2 *Management as a factor of production*[13]
Most of the theoretical literature on international trade deals with labour and capital as the only factors of production, although a few introduce land as a further factor. The mathematical tradition in international trade literature would include management as one of the factors of production in their formal presentations, but we are not aware of any attempts to deal with management systematically as a factor of production in inter-country differences or international trade.

12 These concepts were used in the Wonnacott-Wonnacott (1967) study to estimate the production costs of the tariffs in both countries, and what the potential economic effects of free trade between the United States and Canada would be. Wonnacott and Wonnacott, *Free Trade Between the United States and Canada*, pp. 291-7.
13 It is of interest that only Harry Johnson and one other external reader gave this part of an earlier version any support or encouragement. Four other readers were critical.

In a sense this is not too surprising. Much of traditional price theory makes simplifying assumptions about the behaviour of the firm (and the consumer) and derives implications for the behaviour of prices and quantities in the market. Only limited work has been done by economists on the decision-making process *within* the firm, although the effects of alternative assumptions to profit maximizing have been explored. For our purposes, it is sufficient to point out that the two most comprehensive studies of tariffs in Canada give almost no consideration to management.

The Eastman-Stykolt volume has no reference to management in a 16-page index but has a few sentences in the last paragraph of the conclusion to the chapter on foreign control as follows:

This disproportionate incidence of foreign control is also consistent with an assumption of less innate vigour or competence in Canadian than foreign businessmen, but there is no corroborative evidence for this hypothesis and it is left aside ... Indeed, they (measures imposing discriminatory disadvantages on foreign-controlled firms in Canada) would, if successful, only hide the symptom of inferiority, not its reality. Indeed, they would be based on the admission that native talents are inferior and cannot hold their own in open competition. But if Canadian entrepreneurial talent is really innately inferior, impediments to foreign control only deprive Canadian plants of some of the cost advantages of access to the economies of large firm size and make Canadians poorer, not more capable (Eastman and Stykolt, 1967, 108).

In the Wonnacott-Wonnacott volume, the fullest discussion of management is found in the following two sentences:

One major requirement is sufficient flexibility and imagination by management to recognize and grasp the new opportunities for specialization opened up by freer access to the U.S. market. In short, it is essential that, in the face of a new set of circumstances, Canadian management not 'die of shock' in exaggerated fear of possible injury from U.S. competition (Wonnacott and Wonnacott, 1967, 338).[14]

In light of the unsympathetic response of some reviewers to an earlier draft, it may be useful to outline some aspects of economic performance within the

14 The only other references are to a recognition that differences in education between the United States and Canada could be relevant at the management level (p. 41), and footnote 23, p. 186, which plays down the importance of differences in managerial competence in the two countries! Management is not included in the index.

manufacturing firm, where management has an important role. One of management's key functions is to recruit and train labour, purchase or develop capital equipment for the production operations, accumulate investment funds for working capital and longer-term needs, coordinate production, and develop markets for the output of the firm. They are also critical in the area of change and innovation by providing an environment within the organization that is either open to change, innovation, new products, and the search for new markets, or resistant to new ideas from inside or outside the organization and changing market opportunities. This can be a very important function, even though their number might be only a small part of the labour force.[15]

Differences in the speed of adoption of best-practice techniques and the role of management are clearly important in changes over time and in differences in real income per person employed between countries at a specific time. Although the contribution of labour and capital as factor inputs is recognized in recent empirical work on economic growth, the evidence puts much greater emphasis on the increases in output per unit of input, technological change, and management (Denison and Poullier, 1967; Caves and Associates, 1968). In both the studies of economic growth over time, and in explaining differences in output per person at a particular time, differences in output in relation to total factor inputs are more important than the effects of differences in the stock of capital. The implications of these results from empirical studies of economic growth are insufficiently incorporated into trade theory and Chapter 5 will discuss some results for Canada of technological change in manufacturing.

Management is also given considerable emphasis in the rapidly expanding area of international business. Management decisions in business organizations in individual countries, both multinational and domestically owned and controlled, are heavily influenced by the constraints, both domestic and international (Farmer and Richman, 1971; Richman and Copen 1972). The multinational firms and their management have been both praised as an instrument of change and blamed as a source of exploitation and the absence of meaningful management decision-making in developing countries.[16] In light of the limited attention

15 There is very little data on occupations cross-classified by industry. In the United States, the 1970 data suggest the management group is only 5.4 per cent of the number of those employed in manufacturing, and only 1.6 per cent of all male employed persons (U.S. Department of Commerce, *1970 Census of Population. Subject Report* 7-C, *Occupation by Industry*, Table 1, p. 1). Such sectors as wholesale and retail trade, and finance, insurance and real estate have relatively more 'other managers and administrators' in relation to all employed persons than manufacturing.

16 For a positive view see Harry G. Johnson, 'The Efficiency and Welfare Implications of the International Corporation' in Charles P. Kindleberger, *The International Corporation* (Cambridge: M.I.T. Press, 1970), pp. 35-56, and Richard N. Farmer; *Benevolent*

given in most economic studies in general, and tariff discussions in particular, some evidence on the number and backgrounds of Canadian managers will be summarized, emphasizing comparisons with the United States.

It is important initially to realize how relatively small is the number of persons in the managerial group in Canada, particularly in manufacturing. The most appropriate group from the census is 'other managers and administrators,' who amount to 2 per cent of all occupations with employment income in Canada and 2.3 per cent for Ontario (see Table 7). Furthermore, manufacturing is only about one-fourth of the total economy, but the Canadian data are *not* cross classified by industry and occupation as the American data are. In addition, the occupational definition of managers at the aggregative level is heavily weighted by the small variety store and food outlets operated on a family basis, such as Mac's Milk, McDonald's Hamburgers, etc. An OECD study suggested that the proportion of executives to total numbers employed was larger in the tertiary industries than in manufacturing (OECD, 1963, 58).

Senior executives in the United States have been recruited from a wide background of initial occupations. Two developments have become increasingly important in the backgrounds of managers there. Surveys of the formal levels of education of managers indicate that the proportion of top-level businessmen and executives who have attended and graduated from college increased during the 1950s and 1960s. There has also been a pronounced shift towards younger managers in the United States and this has gone further since a survey in 1952 by Warner and Abegglen (Warner and Abegglen, 1955; Grizzardi, 1966; Daly, 1974, 98-105).

The levels of education are frequently lower among Canadian managers than in the United States, reflecting the historically lower level of formal education here. The proportion of the Canadian labour force with a university degree or a complete high school education has been appreciably lower than in the United States, and this difference is continuing even with the substantially increased enrolment ratios in Canada since the 1950s (Bertram, 1965; Wilkinson, 1966; Walters, 1968, 1970). Canada historically has not put as high a proportion of its

Aggression: The Necessary Impact of the Advanced Nations on Indigenous Peoples (New York: McKay, 1972), while a negative assessment is presented in Stephen H. Hymer and Stephen A. Resnick, 'International Trade and Uneven Development' in Jagdish N. Bhagwati et al., *Trade, Balance of Payments and Growth* (Amsterdam: North Holland, 1971). pp. 473-94 and Stephen Hymer, 'The Multinational Corporation and the Problem of Uneven Development,' in J.N. Bhagwati, ed., *Economics and World Order* (New York: Macmillan, 1971), and some of his other studies. A number of economic nationalists in Canada who are concerned about foreign ownership and control tend to have the negative rather than the positive view of the multinational corporation in Canada and to turn to increased government control and direction of their decisions.

young people through high school and university, although significant increases in provincial and federal expenditures on education at these levels took place during the 1950s and 1960s. Since the end of the 1960s, however, the rate of increase in expenditure on post-secondary education has begun to slow down.

There are also some data to indicate that there has been a relative shortage of highly trained management in Canada. In 1961, only 16 per cent of the major managerial categories in the male labour force in Canada had a university degree, compared with 35 per cent in the United States in 1960 (Daly, 1974, 103 and passim). There has also been a much lower proportion of undergraduate and graduate students taking business administration in Canada than in the United States, as pointed out by the Economic Council of Canada. 'At the first-degree level, U.S. universities have recently been graduating about four times the number of business administration and commerce students produced in Canada per thousand of population ... It has been estimated that at the graduate level for the Master of Business Administration degree, the ratio has been seven to one over recent years.' (Economic Council of Canada, 1968, 43; Von Zur Muehlen, 1971)

Although there is a shift to higher levels of education and training in Canadian management, it began later and has not gone nearly as far as this process has gone in the United States. It is of interest that only 30 per cent of managers over sixty-five years of age in Canada had a college education in 1967, compared with approximately 80 per cent for those forty-four years of age or younger (Daly and Peterson, 1973, 561, 562).

Table 6 shows the career sequences of the top business leaders from the American survey for 1952 by Warner and Abegglen. It also shows comparable but more recent results for Canada. Senior executives surveyed in Canada in 1967 had moved into positions of middle and senior management *much later* in their working lives than in the United States survey taken fifteen years earlier. This suggests much slower movement into managerial positions in Canada, presumably based primarily on seniority and experience with the organization rather than on the formal training and the drive and initiative of younger managers emphasized in management recruiting in the United States.

This emphasis on formal training especially in the relevant skills of management decision-making have facilitated the more rapid development, dissemination, and adoption of new managerial methods in production, information processing, and the organizational aspects of management in the United States. There also seems to be less openness in promotion to managerial positions, greater selection of management from the elites, and more emphasis on ascribed status in Canada. These tendencies, together with a shift into managerial positions later in one's career, could make managers in Canada more traditional and less open to change (Daly and Peterson, 1973, 560-1).

TABLE 6

Comparisons of business leaders' career sequences, selected
occupations (United States (1952) and Canada (1967))

	United States 1952	Canada 1967
First occupation		
Major executive	1	0
Minor executive[1]	10	2
Professional	24	13
Totals of above	35	15
Five years later		
Major executive	6	1
Minor executive	39	14
Professional	21	12
Totals of above	66	27
10 years later		
Major executive	26	12
Minor executive	46	43
Professional	14	9
Totals of above	86	64
15 years later		
Major executive	57	52
Minor executive	26	30
Professional	10	6
Totals of above	93	88

[1] Middle-line supervisor in Canadian study

SOURCES: W. L. Warner and J.C. Abegglen, *Occupational
Mobility in American Business and Industry* (Minneapolis:
University of Minnesota Press, 1955), p. 116; and W.G. Daly, "The
Mobility of Top Business Executives in Canada" (MBA thesis,
University of British Columbia, 1972), p. 68

We shall return to management in the context of the possible influence of
tariffs on the distribution of income later in this section, but it may be useful to
recapitulate some of the implications that can be suggested thus far. First, the
managerial group is a critical one that needs much more study by economists
and political scientists than it has yet received. This arises partly from the
group's key role in the decision-making and managerial role within manufacturing, but they are also important in representations to government on such

TABLE 7

Employment income, managers and administrators and all occupations
(Males, 1970, Ontario and Canada)

Occupation	Total with Employment income	($) Average	($) Median
Ontario			
1 Other managers and administrators	52,685	20,232	18,396
2 All occupations	2,251,115	5,291	4,807
3 Ratio, 1/2	.0234	3.82	3.83
Canada			
1 Other managers and administrators	124,515	18,620	15,896
2 All occupations	6,023,325	6,574	6,106
3 Ratio, 1/2	.0207	2.83	2.60

SOURCE: *Census of Canada, 1971* (Ottawa: Information Canada, 1974 and 1975), pp. 14-1
and 2, 17-71 and 72

policies as tariffs, both directly on behalf of their own firm and indirectly in
such organizations as the Canadian Manufacturing Association and the Chambers
of Commerce. Second, adjustments on the supply side of trained and experienced management to demand changes are bound to be slow even with the
American emphasis on younger managers, but lags in response on the supply side
are even longer in Canada where greater emphasis is placed on experience as the
key for recruitment to senior management positions. Third, the Johnson model
suggested that nationalistic policies would involve a redistribution of income
from the poor to the rich (namely the managers and intellectuals). Table 7 gives
some Canadian data from the 1971 Census for both the national and Ontario
averages. Incomes in the managerial group are between 2½ to 4 times larger than
the incomes for all occupations, a significant difference if the managers were
beneficiaries to some degree. It is of interest that the managers are a somewhat
higher share of all occupations in Ontario, and that the income differential to
managers is greater in Ontario than in Canada as a whole. It is also significant
that managers and administrators are only about 2 per cent of the total, and
manufacturing would be about one fourth of the total. Fourth, the earlier discussion on production differences between the United States and Canada has
suggested that longer runs and increased commodity specialization within firms
and industries would occur if tariffs were reduced. Changes in tariffs would
cause a significant change in the environment within which decisions on production and marketing would be made in Canadian manufacturing, probably threat-
ening older managers with more traditional managerial styles. Resistance to the

possibility of tariff reductions would be understandable, especially when some industries would have costs well above those of potential foreign suppliers.

3 Tariffs and the distribution of income in the short and long run

One of the major sources of confusion in the effects of tariffs is the possibility of a difference between the short-run and long-run determinants of the distribution of income. Michael Mussa has developed this distinction in a recent theoretical paper under a number of important simplifying assumptions (Mussa, 1974). Some of these same distinctions are also relevant to adjustments in employment and production, and this topic will be considered further in the last section in this chapter.

Mussa's basic model was for the two commodity, two factor, one country situation, but did not allow for the tariff to affect production conditions in the industry producing the item, even in the long run. Basically, he used the traditional method of comparative statics to develop the contrasting results of the Marshallian approach (where the supply of one specific factor is taken as fixed while the other factor is mobile) and the longer run (which assumes complete mobility of factors between uses and is related to the Stolper-Samuelson results). All variations of the models assumed full employment of the labour force. A major conclusion is that the long-run interest of one factor can be contrary to its short-run interest.

In the short term, both factors in the protected sector would gain, and the magnitude of the gains would depend on the relative factor intensity in the protected sector relative to the economy as a whole, and the degree to which other factors could be substituted. In the Marshallian tradition, the duration of the time that the factor being used intensively in the protected sector could benefit would depend on the ease and speed of adjustment on the supply side. With time, new firms and the expansion of existing ones could lead to more factors being used in the protected sector (by being shifted out of other industries) and increase the supply of the protected commodity being produced domestically.

In the long term, the distribution of income would be affected not only by the degree of factor intensity in the protected industry (which Mussa emphasizes) but also by the factor supplies and prices in the country imposing the tariff compared to the factor availability and factor prices in its main trading partners, as emphasized by Stolper-Samuelson (1941).[17]

17 Mussa's analysis deals with one country in isolation, emphasizing that in the long run one factor could gain if it were used relatively more intensively in the protected sector, and incorrectly attributes this conclusion to Stolper-Samuelson (ibid., p. 1200). However, the Stolper-Samuelson study dealt with *two* countries and in that situation the scarce factor of production in the country imposing the tariff benefited under protection even if it was not used intensively on the production of the protected commodity.

The major conclusion of the Stolper-Samuelson paper was that the scarce factor of production in the country imposing a tariff could benefit in the long run. Some of the major assumptions in such models in the popular Hecksher-Ohlin tradition would include constant returns to scale, similar production conditions in different countries, no transport costs, international movements of goods, but not factors of production, etc. They also assumed that the country imposing the tariff was relatively small and had no influence on the terms of trade. The model was developed for a two-country, two-commodity situation, but could be extended to more factors of production in certain situations.

It is certainly true that many of these assumptions are not met in assessing international trade between Canada and the United States in the 1970s. For example, Table 3 and the discussion in the last section emphasized the degree to which production conditions (as illustrated by differing levels of real output per person employed in differing manufacturing industries) differed in the two countries. Furthermore, there has been a significant degree of factor mobility between the two countries, in the form of labour (especially in the professional, scientific, and managerial fields), financial capital, and machinery and equipment. The real test of a theory, however, is not in the validity of its assumptions but in the test of its predictions and its possible relevance to new applications. It is in this spirit that it has been introduced.

If one wanted to explore the implications of the Stolper-Samuelson suggestive analysis and conclusions to Canada, how could one assess 'relative scarcity' in practice? One possibility would be to compare factor prices in the two countries. However, the present pattern of factor prices (as well as the structure of relative prices of commodities) in Canada is heavily influenced by the presence of tariffs. For example, machinery and equipment prices have been significantly higher in Canada than in the United States (about 25 per cent in 1965) (Daly, 1968, Table 2, p. 29). However, the presence of tariffs and the manufacturer's sales tax were major factors in that higher price level. In that situation, the higher prices reflected tariff and tax differences and could be a misleading guide to factor supplies in a free (or freer) trade situation. Analogous reasoning has been followed elsewhere in using American relative prices rather than Canadian as a basis of comparing price levels and real income differences, and in weighting the various measures of factor inputs to make a comparison of total factor input in the two countries. It is preferable to use the structure of commodity and factor prices in the large, rather than the small, country as weights for index number comparisons and economic analysis, especially to assess the effects of the reduction of tariff and non-tariff barriers to commodity trade.

The preferable approach would be to use a physical measure of the various factor supplies on a per person employed basis, and this is the route which has been adopted in this study. Under the simplifying assumptions typically made in the Hecksher-Ohlin tradition, these measures of factor supplies and factor prices would be similar. However, if there are significant tax and tariff differences or differences in production conditions between industries, there could be indirect effects on demand conditions for the individual factors of production and the related factor prices and these two criteria need not give the same results. When differences in factor prices do not correspond to the differences in the various factor supplies, some reasons for the possible divergence will be suggested. As a basis of assessing relative factor scarcity, the basic data on physical measures of the various factors of production on a per person employed basis will be used, relying on Dorothy Walters's work on the application of the Denison model of economic growth to Canada.

It should be noted initially that Canada is obviously well endowed with natural resources. The level of arable land per person employed in Canada is roughly double what it is in the United States, while Northwest Europe is about one-sixth the American level on the same basis. Similarly, the value of mineral production per person employed in Canada is about 70 per cent higher than in the United States while Northwest Europe is only about one-fourth the American level (Walters, 1968, 95-8). This is clearly an important source of comparative advantage to Canada, in relation to both the United States and Northwest Europe and has been reflected historically in the composition of Canadian exports. This is clearly an area of relative abundance rather than scarcity and as tariffs on primary products are almost universally lower than on manufactured products, the natural resource side of factor supplies will not be explored further in this study.

What are the implications of these concepts for the possible effects of tariffs on manufactured products on the distribution of income? Let us assume three factors of production: labour (which is relatively mobile between sectors), physical capital (which would be mobile in the long term), and management (whose supply for the economy as a whole changes slowly and also shifts between industries slowly because of the emphasis on seniority and experience in managerial selection in Canada that emerged in the evidence summarized in the last section). Could there be a difference in the short-term and long-term interests for these three factors?

In the short term, labour in manufacturing could benefit from the imposition of a tariff, especially if the product used labour intensively in its production. The higher domestic price for the product (made possible by the tariff) would be partially passed along to the workers in the form of higher wages, which would facilitate the shift of labour into the protected manufacturing sector. This would encourage a higher level of employment in the protected sector, as domestic production expanded to replace goods previously imported.

However, in the long term, as the economy approached a new equilibrium with relatively higher prices for manufactured products, the levels of real income to labour would be lowered absolutely below its real potential. Relatively un-skilled labour tends to be relatively mobile (as reflected in the high turnover rates reflected in data on hirings and separations and gross labour force changes). As a result, it is not to be expected that any non-specific factor could achieve any longer-term gain in the Mussa-type analysis. This is not only the conclusion from theory, but it is bound to occur in practice with the total costs of tariffs of the dimensions discussed in the last section. As labour income amounts to about 80 per cent of net national income in industrialized countries, it is inevitable that a major part of this real cost will fall on this factor of production.

There can be some confusion as to whether the employment effects of a tariff change the composition of employment (more in manufacturing and less in other sectors) or increase total employment.[18] There is little doubt that more employment is generated to produce a given level of output of manufactured products than would be created in the United States (which could be used as a reasonable approximation to a free trade alternative for Canada). However, there are also demand effects to be considered. The aggregate demand for output (including the demand for manufactured products) would be stimulated by the much higher level of real income in the Canadian economy. Demand for manu-factured products would also be stimulated by the decline in manufactured goods prices relative to the prices of other goods and services. Further, there would be important direct and indirect effects on trade in manufactured pro-ducts, as prices of Canadian manufactured goods would fall relative both to other Canadian prices of goods and to prices of manufactured goods produced by Canada's major trading partners. It would be very difficult to assess the extent of this relative price effect in world trade because of the range of countries and commodities that could be involved and the magnitude of the changes would be outside the range of past Canadian experience.

Even if it were correct that a tariff encouraged total employment, rather than just its industrial composition, it would be preferable to use aggregative tools of monetary, fiscal, and exchange rate changes to achieve the desirable levels of resource utilization and high employment, rather than a tariff, which has such clearly adverse effects on real income and resource utilization.[19]

18 Some of this and other sections on the employment implications of tariffs have been added after discussions and correspondence with Abe Rotstein on an earlier draft.

19 It is recognized that significant adjustments in output and employment in manufacturing would be involved in shifting from the present high-cost, low-productivity situation to a more internationally competitive position in manufactured products. The extent of, and need for, such adjustment has been accentuated by the more rapid increase in

It has sometimes been suggested that the Canadian tariff has encouraged a higher level of population and employment than would otherwise be the case, by encouraging the location of manufacturing in Ontario and Quebec. A higher level of population is also encouraged by immigration (Dales, 1966). However, by widening the real income gap between Canada and the United States, the tariff encouraged migration from Canada to the United States, and it is interesting that out-migration to the United States has apparently slowed in recent years, perhaps partly because of the narrowing in real incomes that has been developing. Furthermore, one of the important implications of the Wonnacotts' 1967 volume was that the location of manufacturing in Ontario and Quebec would be *facilitated*, rather than hindered, by free trade. These contradictory assessments of the locational implications of tariffs and free trade were published about the same time and this point will be considered further in the following section.

In light of the relatively lower real labour incomes that have persisted for decades, the high rates of natural increase in the Canadian labour force (especially through the 1960s and 1970s), and the relatively high rates of immigration into Canada (especially during most of the period since World War II), it does not seem appropriate to consider labour as a scarce factor in Canada in the long term. Canada is not really analogous to Australia where the Stolper-Samuelson view that labour could be regarded as the scarce factor of production in the long term has much more validity.

To recapitulate, the Mussa suggestion that the shorter-term and longer-term interests of some factor could diverge does seem to have some relevance to labour in Canada. The tariff could have some stimulative effects on employment and wages in manufacturing when introduced, for the short term.[20] However, the longer-term effects are clearly a lower real income per person employed, while the longer-term effects on total employment and total population are more uncertain. Furthermore, the employment effects, if any in total, could be achieved with less adverse repercussions on real income.

The second factor of production to be considered is durable physical capital assets. Such assets reflect past investment in construction, machinery, and equipment, less capital consumption (covering both physical deterioration with age

money wages and other costs since the late 1960s, the appreciation of the Canadian dollar, and the small narrowing in the manufacturing productivity gap. For a discussion of how to facilitate such adjustments, see the last section of this chapter.

20 Analogous effects in the opposite direction would occur in the transition to lower tariffs or free trade. This may have been a factor in the reservations by some union representatives hinted at in press reports about early drafts of the Economic Council's Commercial Policy Study.

and use, and obsolescence). Income on such assets can be either in the form of profits, or in interest paid. Durable physical assets could achieve a short-term gain in the form of larger profit margins from the imposition of a tariff. However, it is unlikely that this gain could persist for long, unless some other influence apart from the tariff prevented or limited the inflow of new investment and capital assets into the protected sector in the long term. If some barrier to entry existed (such as very large costs for new product development, advertising, or large indivisible units of capital), entry might be difficult and larger profits could persist for a more extended period of time. Legal barriers to entry are limited in manufacturing, however, and the high proportion of approvals of take-overs by the Foreign Investment Review Agency suggests that this new potential limitation on entry is not having a major impact. New and existing firms can initiate production of new products and models relatively easily in Canada and thereby limit any potential high rate of return to profits (or interest) over the longer term. It should be noted that some recent studies have indicated that current production rates are much below potential capacity levels of production and operating rates are further below capacity in recent years than earlier periods, even before the cyclical weakening of 1974-75 in North America (Winston, 1974). Winston pointed out that the capital stock on US manufacturing was idle over 75 per cent of the time, even in the best years. The availability of spare capacity could permit some firms to expand production and limit abnormally high profits relatively easily.

The levels of capital stock per person employed are higher in Canada than in the United States, especially for structures. The data for three broad industry groups are shown in Table 8. The levels of equipment are roughly comparable in agriculture and manufacturing in the two countries, but lower in Canada in the non-agricultural, non-manufacturing sector. North America is clearly much more capital-intensive than Europe. It is interesting that the levels of machinery and equipment per person employed are so similar, particularly when the costs of machinery are much higher relative to labour costs in Canada than they are in the United States. It is possible that some Canadian industries find it cheaper to import and use American machinery than to develop comparable equipment domestically, based on the higher capital to labour costs in Canada. In light of the capital-intensive nature of Canadian production, it does not seem appropriate to class real capital as a scarce factor of production in this country.

In light of the higher levels of fixed capital per person employed in manufacturing and the evidence on rates of return to capital, it is unlikely that capital in manufacturing has had any persisting benefit from the tariff. Such a long-term benefit could persist only if high concentration ratios and significant barriers to

TABLE 8

Canada-U.S. capital stock in U.S. prices per person employed in the
enterprise sectors,* 1960 (Relatives, U.S. = 100)

	Equipment	Structures	Total Fixed Capital
Agriculture	103	156	122
Manufacturing	103	149	123
Other enterprise	63	112	94
All enterprises	79	120	102

*Relatives of the average of gross and net stocks valued in U.S. prices.
Enterprise stocks exclude housing, inventories and land, and general
government and institutional fixed capital.

SOURCE: Dorothy Walters, *Canadian Income Levels and Growth: An
International Perspective*, Staff Study No. 23 for the Economic Council
of Canada (Ottawa: The Queen's Printer, 1968), p. 83

entry were also present at the same time. Furthermore, the high cost, low
productivity conditions that have developed in Canada behind a domestic tariff
would preclude entry into the large, high income market adjacent in the United
States and inhibit long runs, lower costs, and potential export sales there.

Management is the third factor of production to be considered. Like labour,
and capital in manufacturing, management could benefit in the short term from
the imposition of a tariff. Its potential benefit could be relatively greater than
the benefit to the two other factors even in the short term for three possible
reasons. First, the two other factors are fairly similar in Canada and the United
States (in spite of a lower level of formal education and slight differences in age
and sex composition of the labour force and a higher share of construction in
the total stock of capital). On the other hand, there are greater differences in the
age, training, and experience of management in the two countries. Second, the
supply of management in Canada can only be increased at a *slower* rate than
labour or capital. The latter two factors are more readily available or are less
fully utilized (in the case of capital), but management requires more formal
training, or an extended period of experience, which has been emphasized in
past managerial recruitment in Canada. This could make it appropriate to regard
management in Canada an even more fixed and a less variable factor of production than capital (Oi, 1962, for a discussion of recruiting and training
costs in the fixed-variable cost distinction). Third, in relation to net national
income, or total manufacturing cost, managerial income is relatively minute

compared to the returns to labour and capital. Many years ago, Marshall pointed out that this was relevant to the effect of a change in the supply of a factor of production on the extent of price change of that product (Marshall, 1920, 358).

The preceding discussion has suggested that the imposition of a tariff could lead to a short-term gain to the incomes of all factors of production in the protected sector. With the degree of mobility of labour and capital domestically and internationally, it seems unlikely that such gains could persist. However, the small share of managerial incomes in total cost, the long lag in supply response to be expected with the emphasis on experience for promotion to management ranks, and the extent of difference in management backgrounds in the two countries suggest that these gains could persist into the longer term for management to a greater degree than for other factors of production.

4 Some evidence on incomes and income distribution
Earlier sections of this study have set out the analysis as a basis of testing the implications of the Breton-Johnson model to Canadian commercial policy. A number of important points should be made at this stage.

First, the distribution of national income to labour, capital, and land are strikingly similar in the United States, Canada, and the eight countries of Northwest Europe (Denison 1962, 1974; Denison and Poullier, 1967; Daly, 1968, 1972a; Daly and Walters, 1967). Under these circumstances, the differences in *levels* of real income in relation to labour and other factor inputs are bound to be more important than relative income differences. Second, differences in income distribution can arise from a variety of factors operating simultaneously, and it is not necessarily clear that tariffs (Canadian or American or both) are the critical factor in any differences that emerge, especially if the differences were small. Third, the available data in Canada on management are partial and incomplete on both the monetary and non-monetary gains that could potentially accrue from the presence of tariffs.

Recognizing the importance of these qualifications, it nevertheless seems helpful to see how far the analysis can be carried with existing data and sources.

The information on labour income is particularly important, primarily because of the dominant role of labour income in net national income, both for the economy as a whole and for the manufacturing sector. Earlier parts of this monograph have looked at the production effects of tariffs and the differences in the levels of real output per person employed between American and Canadian manufacturing, both in total and for selected individual industries within manufacturing. This section will look at the levels and differentials in real wages in the manufacturing sectors of the two countries[21] (see Table 9). After staying in the neighbourhood of about 80 per cent of the United States level during much of the 1950s and early 1960s, there has been a significant narrowing since about 1966. From 1963 to 1972, the increase in American real weekly earnings was under 7 per cent or 0.7 per cent per year, well under the long-term increase. From 1950 to 1966, for example, the American annual rate of increase had been about 2.25 per cent per year compounded. For the 1963 to 1972 period in Canada the increase was 24 per cent or about 2.5 per cent per year, identical with the rate of increase from 1950 to 1966. The narrowing in real weekly earnings thus primarily reflected a much slower rate of increase in average real weekly earnings in the United States, rather than any acceleration in Canada. The net result is a narrowing in the gap to less than half of what it had been historically, or for the year 1963, the year used in both the West study and the study by Ronald and Paul Wonnacott. The gap is still appreciable between Ontario and Quebec in relation to the adjacent states in the North-eastern United States, and the regional aspects will be considered further later in this chapter.

This narrowing is even more apparent in money wage differences, measured both by average hourly earnings in manufacturing and by average annual labour income in the two countries. This has been emphasized by Harry Waisglass and by one of the publications of the Department of Labour in Ottawa.[22] For some months during 1974 and 1975, average hourly earnings were higher in Canada than in the United States.[23] The maintenance of a gap in weekly earnings, while it has disappeared in hourly earnings, reflects shorter working hours in Canada, amounting to a difference of about 7 per cent in the late 1960s and early 1970s.

21 These estimates are based on average weekly wages of production workers (referred to as 'hourly rated wage-earners only' in Statistics Canada publications), deflated by the consumer price index for each country. An adjustment has been made for a slight difference in the average level of consumer goods and services in each country in 1965. See Appendix by E.C. West in Dorothy Walters, *Canadian Income Levels and Growth: An International Perspective*, Staff Study No. 23 for the Economic Council of Canada (Ottawa: Queen's Printer, 1968), p. 260.

22 Notes for an address to the Conference Board in Canada on Compensation in Canada, Toronto, February 1974, by Harry J. Waisglass, Director-General, Research and Development, Canada Department of Labour and Labour Canada, *Canadian Labour Income: Recent Trends – The Current Picture* (Ottawa: Information Canada, 1974), Tables 19 and 22 and Chart I and K, pp. 45-6, 50, and 52.

23 For a discussion of the narrowing in the May 1974 data, see the *Toronto Star*, September 16, 1974, pp. 1 and A2. A number of newspapers discussed such data in the context of some leaks of the Economic Council study on commercial policy.

This significant narrowing in money earnings (on both an hourly and weekly basis) while the narrowing in real output per person employed has been relatively modest, was facilitated by much greater increases in output per man hour in most of the non-manufacturing industries in Canada than in the United States.[24] In an international trade context, these developments within manufacturing have led to a significant weakening in the competitive position of Canadian manufacturing, relative to the United States. The more rapid increases in labour costs per unit of output and the appreciation of the Canadian dollar since May 1970 are bound to have a delayed effect on trade in manufactured products, especially when wage settlements in Canada in 1975 have been well in excess of those taking place in the United States. In the 1968-70 period, the net trade deficit in highly manufactured products as a percentage of GNP has declined to about 4 per cent, but has widened in 1973-74 (Economic Council of Canada, 1975, 22).

However, for the balance of payments, implications of these developments have been partially offset by high exports of natural resource products and an improvement in the terms of trade during 1973 and 1974, although prices of primary products have weakened with lower levels of industrial output in many of the industrialized countries.

The pattern of manufacturing wage rates, productivity differences, and exchange rates in the latter part of 1975 does not appear to be an equilibrium situation. A maintenance of such a small differential in real weekly earnings in manufacturing between the two countries would require a significant narrowing in the persisting large productivity gap, and changes in commercial policy would seem to be a necessary condition for such a change. Further discussion of these important and interesting questions would take us away from our main theme.

Real incomes of those employed in manufacturing in Canada are lower than in adjacent regions in the United States, primarily because of the presence of tariffs on manufactured products, and some narrowing in the productivity gap seems necessary and desirable if the recent narrowing in real earnings is to be sustained.

Turning to the rate of return of capital, it is of interest that the rates of return to real capital (including both corporate profits taxes in addition to the private return) are no higher in Canada than in the United States. Glenn Jenkins estimated the gross average real rate of return at 9.5 per cent over the period

---

24 See Statistics Canada, *Aggregate Productivity Measures, 1946-1972* (Ottawa: Information Canada, 1974), pp. 22-3 and 49-51; *Statistics Canada Daily*, April 7, 1975, pp. 3-4 and unpublished worksheets from Statistics Canada.

TABLE 9

Real average weekly earnings in manufacturing,
production workers, Canada and United States
(U.S. constant dollars 1961 = 100)

Year	Canada ($)	United States ($)	Canada U.S. (%)
1950	55.70	72.54	76.8
1	56.40	72.89	77.4
2	60.10	75.63	79.5
3	63.36	78.83	80.4
4	64.33	78.50	81.9
5	66.44	84.58	78.6
6	68.75	86.67	79.3
7	69.27	86.80	79.8
8	69.70	85.62	81.3
9	72.34	90.62	79.8
1960	73.31	90.72	80.8
1	74.97	92.34	81.2
2	76.37	95.42	80.0
3	77.73	97.29	79.9
4	79.71	99.30	80.3
5	81.52	101.92	80.0
6	82.84	103.54	80.0
7	85.51	102.96	83.0
8	87.20	105.34	82.8
9	89.64	105.64	84.9
1970	92.93	102.95	99.3
1	98.25	105.17	93.4
2	102.61	110.65	92.7
3	102.33	111.58	91.7
4	102.26	106.79	95.8

SOURCES: Bureau of Labor Statistics, United States
Department of Labor, *Handbook of Labor Statistics*,
various years; Statistics Canada, *Prices and Price
Indexes*, various years; and Statistics Canada, *Review
of Manhours and Hourly Earnings* and *Employment,
Earnings and Hours*, various years

1965-69 in Canada, while the comparable rate was 10.4 per cent in the United States (Jenkins, 1972; Stockfish, 1969)[25] This result is in line with the analysis of the last section, that no long-term difference in return to capital was to be expected as long as there was relatively easy entry for new firms and products, expecially when stocks of real capital assets were relatively high compared with the United States, in relation to both employment and output.

In summary, it seems inappropriate to consider labour, capital, or natural resources as scarce factors of production over the longer term in an international context, either in the present situation of persisting tariff and non-tariff barriers, or in a situation of free trade or lower tariffs. For these factors of production there seems no basis for concluding that the long-term effects of tariffs would improve their real income position. Historically, the only areas where Canada has tended to be relatively *short* of resources have been in certain key areas of *human capital* − highly educated manpower and managerial training and expertise. The importance of this group in company performance, in spite of their small size (as measured by numbers or income shares), has already been discussed and emphasized. It is also of importance that the proportion of the young people obtaining advanced education, especially in relation to business, is still well below the United States in spite of increased expenditures on education over the last two decades. The educational level of the total labour force will change only very gradually since it will take some years for the existing labour force with lower educational levels to be replaced by younger persons with more education.

In what respects could the managers in domestic manufacturing (both foreign-owned and Canadian-owned) benefit by the presence of tariffs in Canada? There are only three ways that such benefits could arise − in the form of higher incomes, in the form of a larger number of managerial jobs in manufacturing or greater responsibility in decision-making, or in the form of less competitive pressure. Each of these possible forms of benefit will be explored, even though the information is fragmentary and suggestive rather than comprehensive and conclusive.

The data on incomes do *not* support the possibility of any financial gain to managers in Canada, although no separate data for management in manufacturing for the two countries have been found. Although N.V. Chapman and Associates survey executive salaries regularly in Canada, they have not made a

25 Similar conclusions had been reached for an earlier period using a different measure of return to capital (namely corporate profits after taxes plus interest paid) in relation to sales and assets in the non-financial corporate sector by industry in work done for the Royal Commission in Banking and Finance. See D.J. Daly, 'Corporation Finance,' mimeo (Ottawa, December 1963). This conclusion also applied to individual industries within manufacturing.

full comparison with the United States. The available data indicate that the salary gap between executive positions in the two countries is somewhat wider than it is for salaried workers or for the economy as a whole. A study by Duncan Campbell concludes that: 'In general the work done to date by a variety of associations and organizations that conduct pretty extensive executive compensation surveys indicate that the Canadian senior manager or executive earns somewhere between 65% and 85% of his U.S. counterpart ... The mean is of the order of 75% for all senior employees across all sizes of organizations.' (Campbell, 1971).[26] Since there is no way of ensuring that the qualifications of those surveyed were comparable, the income differences could be a mixture of quality and price differences. The evidence suggests, however, that any gain from the presence of tariffs probably does not accrue in a financial form.

Another form in which managers could benefit from the tariff is in the form of relatively more managerial type jobs than would otherwise exist. Since the managerial group is small and census data are not broken down by industry in Canada, this cannot be assessed directly. However, in this chapter, it was pointed out that there are relatively more plants (some of which are less than optimum size) in some industrial sectors in Canada than in the United States, relative to the respective domestic markets. This is reflected in smaller average plant size in Canada (Eastman and Stykolt, 1967; Scherer, 1973, 135). Company sizes in manufacturing are also smaller on average, with fewer plants per company in Canada than in the United States (Rosenbluth, 1957, Ch. IV; Caves, 1975). These differences in company and plant sizes are presumably related to relatively more management positions in Canada, although the evidence is admittedly indirect rather than direct. It should also be noted that the pattern of a relatively large number of small plants in individual manufacturing industries in the United States is not observable in Canada to anything like the same extent. In a large market like the United States, it is possible for a small plant to be quite efficient and profitable, producing and selling a limited range of parts or components to larger firms in the same broad industry. However, the much smaller, protected Canadian market is too small to absorb longer runs of a few product items. Under free trade, it is possible that many more small firms and plants would develop in Canada to serve the whole North American market and market size would cease to be a significant limiting factor as it has been. However, the availability of the managerial and scientific manpower could then become even more critical.

26 This is gross earnings before tax. The *marginal* tax rates under the personal income tax are higher in Canada than in the United States, after considering taxes at both the federal and provincial (or state) levels, especially in the $20,000 income range. The American split income provision and different treatment of housing and various tax credits are important in this difference (Daly, 1970).

A third form in which management in Canada could benefit from the tariff would be in the form of more leisure and less competitive pressure, a possibility raised by Harry Johnson. Although this is a plausible hypothesis consistent with other material, there does not seem to be any information or evidence to test the possibility in any depth. It is an area for further study and research.

To summarize, the above analysis of the tariff corresponds fairly well with Johnson's model from his analysis of the developing countries. It has clearly led to a lower level of net national income per person employed, higher prices for manufactured products to the consumer, and lower real incomes to the workers in manufacturing in the long although not necessarily in the short term. Any benefits in the long term can accrue only to the managerial group, although presumably in the form of more employment opportunities, more leisure, and less competitive pressure. The lessened competitive pressure can occur in the form of less price competition and less pressure to innovate or adopt new technology (as will be developed further in Chapter 5). As managers have incomes above the average income earner and the incidence of the tariff is regressive by income group, this implies that the costs fall on lower income groups and the non-financial benefits accrue to those with above average incomes. As has already been mentioned, the data suggest that managers have had less formal training to carry out their managerial functions and have moved into middle and senior levels of management later in their professional careers than in the United States.

In an excellent recent study of equality and efficiency, Arthur Okun expresses a willingness to give up some gains in efficiency and total output to gain additional equality (Okun, 1975). However, the effects of tariffs on Canada clearly involve costs in efficiency borne largely by consumers and urban workers while the long-term benefits accrue primarily to a relatively small, high income group. Such results are adverse on both efficiency and equality criteria.

This raises the question of how a small minority has been able to benefit from government economic policies in a democracy. Partly it is a matter of insufficient understanding by the general public and affected groups of the costs and benefits of tariffs. However, it is also true that the costs of tariffs as estimated in the study by Ronald and Paul Wonnacott for 1963 and by Ronald Wonnacott for 1974 are large in relation to GNP, but the costs are widely spread and are not dramatic per adult consumer or per worker in manufacturing. It is not worth a lot of time for an individual consumer or urban worker to write his Member of Parliament, a cabinet minister, or a civil servant about the tariff. However, it could be quite important for a middle-level or senior manager to take an active interest in protecting the existing corporate strategy and his personal function in a protected environment. This interpretation is consistent with recent work on the economic theory of democracy (Downs, 1957). The notion that government regulation in other fields usually ends up protecting the producer rather than the consumer has been well documented (Stigler, 1971; Jordan, 1972).

The implications of these notions for decision-making in Canada would be worth further study, incorporating material by John Porter and Wallace Clement on élites, and Robert Presthus on élites in Canada and the United States (Porter, 1965; Clement, 1975; Presthus, 1973).

REGIONAL DISTRIBUTION OF THE TARIFF

The primary interest of this study is the influence of tariffs on real national income per person employed and per capita; little attention is being given to the movement of resources between countries and regions. This section shifts from the earlier concern about tariffs as an illustration of economic nationalism in Canada-United States income differences to the regional implications of the presence of tariffs and the possible effects of their removal.

Before considering the role of tariffs in regional disparities, it should be noted that economists and statisticians have thus far been much less successful in explaining the main factors that have contributed to the persisting inter-regional income differences within Canada, whether on a per person employed or a per capita basis. A number of studies have described the size of income differences and some important factors have been identified, but the degree of real understanding is still limited and progress has been slow in spite of more professional resources and more regional data.[27] The lack of understanding of the reasons for persisting regional income disparities is bound to affect policies proposed and adopted to deal with these disparities.

These comments on the regional distribution of tariffs will follow the same order as the earlier discussion at the national level.

The level of prices of manufactured goods is higher in Canada because of Canadian tariffs, both relative to prices of manufactured goods in the United States and other goods and services within Canada. Prices of manufactured goods would decline if Canadian tariffs were reduced, falling more in line with prices of the United States or any other low-cost supplier, and prices of manufactured products would drop relative to prices of services and food. Such a result would occur irrespective of whether the Canadian tariffs were reduced on a unilateral, bilateral, or multilateral basis. There is no reason to expect the relative price declines in manufactured products to be any different from one region to another.

27 Earlier staff studies by Isabel Anderson, S.E. Chernick, and Frank Denton for the Economic Council of Canada illustrate some of the work done during the 1960s.

Ronald Shearer has made an estimate of the direct gains of a North Atlantic free trade area to the residents of British Columbia of 5.5 per cent of personal income (Shearer, Young and Munro, 1973, 201). This is much less than the Wonnacott-Wonnacott estimate in the 1967 volume or the revised estimate by Ronald Wonnacott in the 1975 volume for the Economic Council of Canada. In explanation of the smaller relative size of the British Columbia estimates than for Canada, Shearer points out that the dislocations and adjustments (as well as the gains) would be smaller in British Columbia than in Ontario and Quebec: 'North Atlantic free trade would raise incomes in the industrialized regions of Canada relative to incomes in areas like British Columbia. Free trade would be less of a stimulus to economic expansion in British Columbia than in the industrialized central part of the country.' (Shearer, Young, and Munro, 1973, 203).

The estimate considers the costs to consumers, costs to producers, effects of lower tariffs in other countries on export industries in British Columbia, and internal redistributions within Canada, and the qualifications to the estimates are emphasized. Surprisingly, however, there is no discussion of the changed production conditions associated with the presence of or removal of tariffs, and no allowance for this is made in the quantitative sections (Shearer, Young, and Munro, 1973, 179-82, 202). It is unlikely that this could be relatively as important in British Columbia as in central Canada, but the omission is striking, bearing in mind the care that had gone into the theoretical sections and industry descriptions.

As discussed earlier, the existence of the tariff, even at lower rates, was reflected in the lower levels of output per person employed in Canadian manufacturing as compared with those in the United States. These lower levels of productivity were particularly relevant to a consideration of manufacturing, which is heavily concentrated in Ontario and Quebec.

A related aspect of this productivity gap is the lower level of real weekly earnings in Ontario and Quebec than in the adjacent states in the northeastern United States.[28] This can be seen in Table 10 for Ontario and Table 11 for

28 There are twenty states within 400 miles of the manufacturing belt in Ontario between Windsor and Cornwall, whose personal income and population will be examined in considering the market potential under free trade later in this section. The six most populous industrialized states in that region are Illinois, Indiana, Michigan, New York, Ohio, and Pennsylvania. Average weekly earnings in those states have been combined to make a weighted average with fixed weights with the number of employees in 1961 as a base. The United States consumer price index was used to deflate average weekly earnings to these six states, and the Canadian index was used for Ontario. This procedure assumes that the purchasing power of $1 in income in Ontario was equal to $1 in income in the United States. From the price comparisons at the national level, done by Statistics Canada in 1965, this is probably not inappropriate.

Quebec. In the early 1950s, the earnings level in Ontario was about 25 per cent lower than in the adjacent northeastern states, and the gap had narrowed to about half that early in the 1970s. In Quebec, the gap has always been greater, about 35 per cent in 1950 and narrowing to about 25 per cent in 1972. Thus the Ontario gap has been smaller during the last twenty-five years or so, and has narrowed more in recent years than in Quebec.

It might be noted that the gaps shown in Tables 10 and 11 are wider in recent years for Ontario and Quebec relative to adjacent states than the differences for total manufacturing at the national level shown in Table 9 earlier. The northeastern states have always had weekly earnings in manufacturing above the United States national average. In 1950, average weekly earnings of production workers in these states had been about 6 per cent above the national average, and by 1972 the difference had widened to almost 12 per cent.

Average weekly earnings in current dollars are shown in Table 12 for the five regional groupings which have been considered in this study. As can be seen, Ontario by 1972 had weekly earnings almost equal to the United States national average, but still below the adjacent states in the northeast. Quebec is still appreciably below both the adjacent states and the American national average.

A view of the tariff frequently held in most regions of Canada is that individuals in the Prairies, British Columbia, and the Maritimes bear the cost of higher prices, but that labour in Ontario and Quebec benefit. The data and analysis above, for Canada and Ontario and Quebec, indicate that real wages are lower than in the adjacent parts of the United States, although the gap has begun to narrow since about 1966. Important in these real wage differences are the differences in real output per person employed at the national level, and the role that tariffs and non-tariff barriers to trade have played in the performance of Canadian manufacturing.

What would the elimination or further reductions in tariffs in both Canada and the United States (either bilaterally or as part of a multilateral settlement) do to the remaining real wage differences? It would certainly require greater adjustments within Canada than within the United States, reflecting the greater potential gains to Canada than to the United States,[29] and the large gap shown in the data from the study by E.C. West included in Table 3. However, earlier interviews suggest that the adjustments on the production side are not that difficult, given the willingness on the part of management to make the adjustment. Basically what is required is a rationalization of production through dropping low margin items, frequently involving short runs. The same labour and

29 The estimate of the gains to Canada in 1963 was 10.5 per cent of GNP, while the estimate of the gain to the United States was expected to be well under 1 per cent of GNP (Wonnacott and Wonnacott, 1967, 301).

TABLE 10

Real average weekly earnings in manufacturing, production
workers, Ontario and six northeastern States
(U.S. constant dollars, 1961 = 100)

Year	Ontario ($)	Six N.E. States ($)	Ontario / Six N.E. States (%)
1950	57.96	76.83	75.44
1	58.57	77.64	75.44
2	62.46	80.56	77.53
3	65.78	84.73	77.63
4	66.62	84.18	79.14
5	68.98	91.02	75.79
6	71.42	93.55	76.34
7	72.13	93.40	77.23
8	72.40	91.71	78.94
9	75.71	98.10	77.18
1960	76.58	98.23	77.96
1	78.45	99.46	78.88
2	80.01	103.09	77.61
3	81.66	205.49	77.41
4	83.82	108.41	77.32
5	85.99	111.75	76.95
6	86.54	112.53	76.90
7	88.02	110.92	79.35
8	91.07	114.39	79.61
9	93.59	114.59	81.67
1970	97.67	115.55	84.53
1	103.32	115.92	89.07
2	107.51	123.39	87.12
3	108.00	125.01	86.39

SOURCES: Bureau of Labor Statistics, United States Department of
Labor, *Employment and Earnings, States and Areas*, various years;
Statistics Canada, *Prices and Price Indexes*, various years; and
Statistics Canada, *Review of Manhours and Hourly Earnings* and
Employment, Earnings and Hours, various issues

capital can produce much larger outputs if long runs rather than short runs are
produced, and the experience in Canada under the Canada-United States auto
agreement and the experience under the Common Market and EFTA regional
arrangements for free trade in industrial products illustrate the realism of that
analysis. Although it is apparently not profitable for individual firms and industries

TABLE 11

Real average weekly earnings in manufacturing, production
workers, Quebec and six Northeastern States
(U.S. constant dollars, 1961 = 100)

Year	Quebec ($)	Six N.E. States ($)	Quebec / Six N.E. States (%)
1950	51.57	76.83	67.12
1	52.06	77.64	67.05
2	55.52	80.56	68.92
3	58.32	84.73	68.83
4	59.19	84.18	70.31
5	60.98	91.02	67.00
6	63.29	93.55	67.65
7	60.07	93.40	64.31
8	63.43	91.71	69.16
9	65.35	98.10	66.62
1960	66.75	98.23	67.95
1	68.32	99.46	68.68
2	69.69	103.09	67.60
3	70.58	105.49	66.91
4	72.23	108.41	66.63
5	73.20	111.75	65.50
6	75.63	112.53	67.21
7	76.96	110.92	69.38
8	79.38	114.39	69.39
9	81.33	114.59	70.97
1970	83.67	115.55	72.41
1	87.31	115.92	75.32
2	89.74	123.39	72.43
3	89.32	125.01	71.45

SOURCES: Bureau of Labor Statistics, United States Department
of Labor, *Employment and Earnings, States and Areas,* various
years; Statistics Canada, *Prices and Price Indexes,* various years;
and Statistics Canada, *Review of Manhours and Hourly Earnings*
and *Employment, Earnings and Hours,* various issues

in Canada to specialize in the environment of existing tariff structures, it would
be essential to specialize and narrow the cost and productivity differences under
free or freer trade. The reductions in tariff rates on capital goods and intermediate
productions and the related specialization in domestic-supplying industries would
lead to reductions in costs of purchased materials, both domestic and imported.

TABLE 12

Average weekly earnings in manufacturing, production workers, 1972,
current dollars selected regions, Canada and United States

	Current dollars, domestic currencies	U.S. = 100
Quebec	$125.79 Can.	81.32
Canada average	141.47 Can.	91.45
Ontario	150.32 Can.	97.17
United States average	154.69 U.S.	100.00
Northeastern States (weighted average, 6 largest)	172.50 U.S.	111.51

SOURCES: Bureau of Labor Statistics, United States Department of
Labor, *Employment and Earnings, States and Areas*, various years;
Statistics Canada, *Prices and Price Indexes*, various years; and Statistics
Canada, *Review of Manhours and Hourly Earnings* and *Employment,
Earnings and Hours*, various issues

What would the market outlets be for the increased output of manufactured products from Ontario and Quebec plants? Unquestionably, an important part of that output could most easily be sold in the adjacent states of the northeastern United States. Within a 400-mile radius of the manufacturing belt from Windsor to Cornwall there are twenty states, many of them densely populated and high income areas.[30] In 1970, that region contained 104 million people and the level of non-farm personal income in 1972 was just under $500 billion (U.S. Dept. of Commerce, 1973). This is roughly five times the total Canadian population at that time, and more than six times the total Canadian level of non-farm personal income of 1972 (Statistics Canada, 1974, 18, 21).[31] A 400-mile radius would locate these states within a reasonable overnight truck drive from the manufacturing centres of Ontario. The same distance would be applicable if the region were used as a source of supply of components, professional advice, managerial expertise, etc. A Canadian plant would need only to penetrate a number of adjacent states to have a market comparable to a much more

30 The twenty states included are Maine, New Hampshire, Vermont, Massachusetts, Rhode Island, Connecticut, New York, New Jersey, Pennsylvania, Delaware, Maryland, District of Columbia, Michigan, Ohio, Indiana, Illinois, Wisconsin, Virginia, West Virginia, and Kentucky. There are some differences in personal income per capita within this group, with parts of New England and the area south and west of Washington, D.C., being below the regional average.
31 The level of non-farm personal income in 1972 was $80.2 billion compared with $498.8 billion in the twenty northeastern states in the same year.

heterogeneous and scattered domestic market with typically lower average incomes domestically.

Quebec is not quite as well situated as Ontario in relation to these states. The states of Delaware, Indiana, Illinois, Kentucky, Maryland, Michigan, Ohio, Virginia, West Virginia, Wisconsin, and the District of Columbia are all more than 400 miles away. The nine states within 400 miles had a population of 49 million (well above the Canadian total but less than half that of the 20 states within 400 miles of Ontario) and a total of non-farm personal income of $245 billion in 1972 (U.S. Dept. of Commerce, 1973a, 1-48; 1973b, 32-3). On the other hand, Quebec does have a lower wage level than Ontario, well below the average of the adjacent states, and thus can be a source of industrial location for low wage industries, if higher wage industries do not locate there.

The presence of tariffs and non-tariff barriers to the flow of trade in manufactured products has important implications for Ontario and Quebec manufacturing. It is not just the presence of tariffs in the United States that limits exports or reduces the prices to potential exporters who have to absorb the American tariff to sell there, a point that most Canadians accept. The presence of a Canadian tariff encourages higher prices for manufactured products and high cost, low productivity within domestic manufacturing. Even if American tariffs were eliminated, the continuance of Canadian tariffs would permit a continuance of high domestic costs and domestic producers would not be sufficiently competitive in the United States market. Finally, an important long-term result of free trade would be a further increase in real income to the urban worker in Ontario and Quebec.

These conclusions are similar to those arrived at by Ronald and Paul Wonnacott on location pressures in a free trade area.

There is a central industrial heartland in the North American continent. This may be roughly defined by drawing a triangle from Chicago to the West of Boston and Washington, the two terminal points of the band of heaviest industrial activity along the eastern seaboard ... This 'North American Triangle' represents only slightly more than five percent of the area of the United States, and about two and one half percent of the area of the North American continent. Nevertheless, approximately thirty percent of the population of Canada and the United States is in this area ... This area includes only a small Canadian section – the southernmost strip of southwestern Ontario. Toronto and Montreal lie just to the north.

In terms of many of the location influences considered [earlier], it is a superior region for several reasons. It is the area of heaviest central location of industry; as a consequence, it is attractive both for firms that may be drawn by external economies to concentrations of firms in their own industry and for firms seeking best sources of a wide variety of manufactured supplies. Because it is the area of heaviest industrialization, it is also the area of greatest concentration of employment and income. Firms seeking rich markets find it attractive as a consequence ... The concentration of markets in this area along with its fairly central location together ensure that this region is one of the best areas from which to service North American markets at minimum transport costs. These advantages have allowed firms in this area, competing with firms less favorably situated elsewhere, to pay higher wages ...

The same reasons that make the regions in this triangle most attractive also make the regions that are adjacent to them the next most attractive location. Hence, the next most favored areas are the Canadian provinces of Ontario and Quebec, lying along the northern border of this triangle (Wonnacott and Wonnacott, 1967, 146, 147, 151).

On the basis of the various criteria and the relative wage levels and exchange rate of the 1960s, they conclude that: 'The Canadian industrial complex in the Windsor-Quebec City area would be very favorably situated for expansion in most industrial sectors in the event of free trade. The implication is that the long-run process of international adjustment would involve some rise in Canadian wages relative to U.S. wages or an appreciation of the Canadian dollar or both' (Wonnacott and Wonnacott, 1967, 163).

It is interesting that this conclusion published in 1967 has been partially realized already, with the narrowing in real wage differences shown in Tables 10 and 11 earlier, and the appreciation of the Canadian dollar since it was permitted to float in June 1970. How much of these changes are a reflection of the tariff reductions made under the Kennedy Round (and since implemented) and the Canada-United States automotive agreement, and how much is attributable to other factors, is difficult to disentangle.

Some earlier studies of the Canadian tariff have concluded that the tariff encouraged a larger population in Ontario and Quebec, although recognizing that it involved lower real incomes per capita.[32] Historically, Canadian population movements internationally were dominated by an inflow of immigrants from Europe (and from other continents in more recent years) and an outflow to the

32 John Dales, *The Protective Tariff in Canada's Development* (Toronto: University of Toronto Press, 1966) discusses this and includes some discussion of the role of factor movements and immigration in the analysis of the tariff. Roma Dauphin emphasizes the lower degree of labour mobility in Quebec in his study, *The Impact on Quebec of Canadian and American Tariffs*. Dr Mackintosh also considers population size in his study for the Rowell-Sirois Report.

United States. A narrowing in real wage and income differences between Canada and the United States would be reflected in some slowing in the net migration to the south.

Our assessment has put greater emphasis on real wage differences and national income per person employed, as these are key and preferable measures of economic welfare. Population size, per se, seems less important as a guide to performance and economic policy. It is also difficult to assess the longer-term pattern of industrial location in Ontario and Quebec. The above analysis has been more optimistic on the future of Ontario and Quebec manufacturing than some earlier studies. A key factor in the response of the economy to further reductions in tariffs is the response of Canadian businessmen to a changed and more competitive environment. An attempt to retain something close to the historical pattern of short runs and high-cost production, with sales limited to a small domestic market, would lead to an erosion of profit margins and increased difficulties. Specialization, long runs, and increased exports to the adjacent American markets, as well as to the rapidly growing markets in Europe and Japan, would shift Canada into the world market for manufactured products. The adaptability of management and willingness to adopt new ideas, new products, and new production methods are critical.

The tariff as an illustration of economic nationalism has in the past contributed to higher prices to Canadian consumers and lower real incomes to the urban worker in Ontario and Quebec. Key in the decision to continue past policies or to shift to a more competitive, specialized, and productive manufacturing sector is the attitude of the small but important sector of management in manufacturing and their attitude to corporate strategy and tariff policy.

In the next section, a number of policy considerations will be reviewed; these are somewhat tangential but relate to the main theme of the tariff and economic nationalism.

RELATED POLICY IMPLICATIONS

The earlier sections have outlined the costs to the consumer and the urban worker in manufacturing of economic nationalism in the form of tariffs in Canada and the United States. It has also been suggested that management and the professional group in manufacturing are the primary beneficiaries of the tariff, relatively small in numbers and a relatively scarce segment, but a key group in decision-making within the organization.

The persistence of tariffs for decades has had an important impact on the structure of Canadian manufacturing and its performance, and the related system of distribution. No changes in such a complex and interrelated system can be made overnight, and changes would have effects in many other related areas. This section will recapitulate some major conclusions in these areas to assure the reader that they have been recognized and considered, without attempting a complete assessment of all the considerations.

The first three points all deal with policy measures that would facilitate any adjustments on the employment side that could arise. It might be helpful, initially, to talk about their extent, as there are persisting differences about the source and extent of such adjustments. It is helpful to distinguish stages in the adjustment process, recognizing that in practice all of these could be occurring simultaneously. In the initial impact, the companies and industries would still be producing on the tariff-protected basis, without the gains from lower prices and higher real incomes domestically. In the intermediate term, companies and industries would have shifted to a greater degree of specialization in domestic production and a much enlarged two-way flow of trade. In the long term, interregional adjustments from factor migration, both within Canada and internationally, would be allowed for (Economic Council of Canada, 1975, 166-71 ff.; Shearer et al., 1973, 47-65, 176). Earlier sections of this monograph have dealt with the effects of tariffs on production, real incomes, and income distribution, and the potential gains once the adjustments in production and marketing under changed commercial policies have been made. It is recognized that the transition from the present high-cost, low-productivity situation will involve extensive changes within Canadian manufacturing.

The next few pages will discuss a number of important supplementary steps to facilitate these necessary adjustments. However, before considering these measures, it might be desirable to consider the extent of the possible adjustments under some extreme assumptions, drawing on recent simulations by the Economic Council of Canada using the CANDIDE model. The changes in manufacturing and in the total economy that would be involved in both unilateral reductions by Canada and bilateral reductions with the United States were compared with the 1969 situation without trade liberalization. The extreme assumptions were made that no reorganization within Canadian manufacturing would occur, that no demand stimulus would occur from higher real incomes domestically, or that a shift in expenditures would occur towards manufactured products because of a decline in their relative prices. Even under these conditions, and with no adjustments in government expenditures, the difference in levels of GNE and domestic output were under one per cent, and less than 2 per cent for manufacturing output. Declines were larger for unilateral reductions in Canadian tariffs alone. In general, the magnitudes of effects were sufficiently small that offsetting changes in fiscal policy — especially with a flexible exchange rate – could keep the extent of adjustments to moderate proportions (Economic Council of Canada, 1975, Table 13-1, p. 168).

If the adjustments in domestic production in the direction of increased specialization, the accompanying reduction of manufactured goods prices domestically and in relation to suppliers in other countries, and higher real incomes within Canada were allowed for, the extent of adverse employment effects would be even less. Much depends on the ease and speed of adjustment within manufacturing, and the willingness of the key managerial group in plants and firms within Canada to encourage the changes in corporate strategy required by the new commercial policy environment.

This monograph emphasizes the intermediate term effects of tariff and non-tariff barriers to trade and their removal, with a brief discussion of how the necessary short-term adjustments could be facilitated. Little attention is given to the long-term adjustments with full mobility of labour and capital inter-nationally. In the situation of the early 1960s, central Canada was a desirable industrial location for new manufacturing plants when wages were significantly lower than in adjacent parts of the northeastern United States and the Canadian dollar was at a significant discount. The potential benefits are less clear now that the wage difference at the national level has disappeared and has narrowed significantly in relation to adjacent key manufacturing states. Plant location under the differing wage and exchange rate pattern of the mid-1970s has not been re-examined, especially from the viewpoint of the multinational cor-poration (which really means the United States parent company).

1 *Adequate internal demand*
Many people in Canada might be concerned about maintaining an adequate level of employment in Canada during the adjustment period to lower tariffs, par-ticularly in light of the evidence on high costs and low productivity levels in secondary manufacturing. This question should certainly be given serious atten-tion by the government during the transition period, but it is a concern that can be met.

For one thing, the government should give priority to a high level of effective final demand during this period. Although monetary and fiscal policy do not work quickly and there are political and administrative problems in making major changes, these aggregative tools can facilitate such adjustments. (For a discussion of monetary and fiscal tools in the context of demand fluctuations, see Daly, 1966, 1972c, 1969, 45-65.) Shifts of resources, particularly manpower, can be more easily made from regions and industries providing low incomes to higher income alternatives during periods of high levels of demand and employ-ment than during periods of slack demand and underutilization.

A high level of effective demand is particularly important as Canada has been experiencing one of the most rapid increases in labour force growth of any of the major industrialized countries since the mid-1960s. For example, the growth is expected to be about 2.7 per cent per year during the 1970s, compared with 1.9 per cent in the United States.

2 *Timing of tariff reductions*
It is recognized that greater adjustments to tariff reductions would have to be made in Canada than in other countries, most of which are already producing for a large free trade market or have lower ratios of trade to GNP than Canada. Plants and firms in Canada need time to adjust corporate strategies to shift away from the existing product diversity and some suboptimal plant sizes producing in a small protected market to more specialized product lines in a larger market. Canada should be permitted to reduce its tariffs over a longer period of time to allow for the domestic adjustments to be initiated, while reductions by other countries could be made over a shorter period of time (Canadian-American Committee, 1965; Wonnacott and Wonnacott, 1968, 307-22).

3 *Facilitating the transition*
Although there was a significant gap in productivity between Canadian and American manufacturing early in the 1960s, an important part of the adjustment could be made within Canada by reducing the degree of product diversity, specializing in a much smaller number of lines, models, and products, and selling the longer runs in adjacent parts of the United States and world market. The result would be a much greater degree of intra-industry specialization (Grubel and Lloyd, 1975). The extent of adjustment that takes place along these lines is dependent to an important degree on the adaptability of management. Whole plants and industries are unlikely to disappear in Canada unless poor management, poor location, or other factors contribute to persisting low profitability, even in a much enlarged potential market.

It is relevant that complete free trade in manufactured products has been achieved within the Common Market (about 190 million people with the initial six countries and 250 million with the proposed nine countries). This process has taken place with lower levels of unemployment and much larger increases in manufacturing productivity than has occurred in North America. The increases in productivity have been so great that they were able to offset an important part of the increases in wages, and only moderate increases in export prices occurred. There have been few reports of bankruptcies in European manufacturing firms with the move to free trade within Europe.

It is also interesting that the Canada-United States free trade agreement in automobiles and automotive products has led to more specialization, a narrowing (and perhaps elimination) of the productivity gap in manufacturing, a narrowing in the wage gap, and a significant net increase in automotive trade – with the increase being greater for Canada. The initial production safeguards have been exceeded and seem no longer to serve any useful purpose. The limited number of producers and the availability of an efficient distribution system through the parent companies in the United States have facilitated the adjustment in this industry, but the operation of the agreement indicates the potential benefits of specialization (Wonnacott and Wonnacott, 1967, 226-47, 341-87; Beigie, 1970, 1972).[33]

Most observers would also recommend additional steps to facilitate the adjustment process. Arrangements for retraining of workers and financing of moving expenses to new jobs have been proposed (Matthews, 1971, 65-80; Baldwin and Mutti, 1973). Some of these measures could assist shifts of workers in the labour market, irrespective of the initial sources of surpluses and shortages, rather than being used only if primarily a result of commercial policy changes. Financial assistance to companies for plant expansion has also been suggested. Canada introduced some steps along these lines while the Kennedy Round reductions were being implemented, and there seems to be general agreement that they are desirable, if only to provide reassurances for those who are pessimistic about the feasibility of Canadian industry making the necessary adjustments. Finally, in light of the emphasis in earlier sections about the role of management, it would also be desirable to give special attention to management education and to continuing education of existing management to facilitate adjustment to future reductions in tariff and non-tariff barriers to trade.

4 Degree of competition

It is recognized that Canadian industry and finance are relatively highly concentrated, to a greater degree than in the United States (Rosenbluth, 1957; Bain, 1966, 103-6). The presence of the tariff, which lowers the degree of price competition from foreign sources of supply, together with a greater degree of concentration, reduces the amount of price competition within Canada. The evidence suggests that a combination of *both* high tariffs and high concentration ratios leads to both higher relative prices and higher relative costs in Canada than in the United States, as shown in Tables 13 and 14. In his paper from which these tables are taken, Harry Bloch draws some interesting implications for government policy.

33 A greater share of the improved performance could have been passed along to the consumer than has occurred thus far. An extension of free trade from existing manufacturers to automotive dealers and consumers would quickly narrow the existing price differences to the consumer, apart from tax differences. Reliable reports of Canadian-produced cars selling in the United States at lower prices than in Canada persist.

TABLE 13

Indexes of Canadian prices divided by U.S. prices, manufacturing industries grouped by concentration and tariff classes

		Concentration classes	
		Low	High
Tariff rates	Low	101.6	104.4
	High	99.8	111.6

SOURCE: Harry Bloch, 'Prices, Costs and Profits in Canadian Manufacturing: The Influence of Tariffs and Concentration, *Canadian Journal of Economics*, November 1974, Table 1, p. 601

TABLE 14

Indexes of Canadian direct cost per unit divided by U.S. direct cost per unit, *manufacturing industries grouped by concentration and tariff classes*

		Concentration classes	
		Low	High
Tariff rates	Low	105.9	100.3
	High	102.8	119.3

SOURCE: Harry Bloch, 'Prices, Costs and Profits in Canadian Manufacturing: The Influence of Tariffs and Concentration,' *Canadian Journal of Economics*, November 1974, Table 3, p. 607

When a Canadian industry has both high tariff duties on imports and high concentration of sales among domestic producers, the prices charged by the Canadian firms relative to the prices charged by their U.S. competitors are on average seven to twelve percent higher than when a Canadian industry has either low concentration or low tariffs or both ... Our findings lead us to speculate that either a competition policy which reduces the concentration of sales among domestic producers or a tariff policy which lowers the Canadian tariffs on imports will lead to lower prices in Canadian manufacturing industries which currently have both high concentration and high tariffs ... We expect that competition policy will have a significant downward influence on profit per unit, while tariff policy will have a significant downward influence on cost per unit (Bloch, 1974, 608, 610).

Milton Moore has made a number of useful suggestions on how to achieve a more effective competition policy in Canada, including more rationalization through reduction in the number of companies and smaller plants through mergers, more price competition at the wholesale and retail levels, and removal of the exemption from combines law for the service industries (Moore, 1970). However, the Moore volume assumed the continuation of tariff protection for secondary manufacturing, suggesting that 'It would be the best part of wisdom for a Canadian government to encourage mergers among Canadian companies as the precursor to the negotiations of free trade, should the policy decision ever be made (Moore, 1974, 129). It is far from clear that mergers would be very important in reducing costs, and it is very doubtful that the government has an adequate basis for deciding what mergers would reduce costs and increase productivity, or merely further increase the already high costs per unit in highly concentrated industries with high tariff rates. It is very doubtful that the persisting gaps in productivity and costs can be narrowed by government policy in the absence of major changes in commercial policy. Moore is clearly concerned about the increased foreign ownership and reduced Canadian independence that he feels could follow from free trade. The emphasis in this monograph is that changes in commercial policy are a necessary, but not a sufficient, condition for a more competitive and efficient Canadian economy, and that a more effective competition policy is a necessary accompaniment to revisions in commercial policy. It is very doubtful that competition policy could be effective in reducing costs in isolation, even if tariff changes were eventually to be made.

5 *Basis of political decision-making*
The persistence of tariffs in Canada reflects the greater influence of senior management on political decision-making, rather than that of the much more numerous urban workers or the large number of relatively unorganized consumers. Personal contacts between the business community and the government and many shared values facilitate an influence of manufacturing management out of all proportion to their numbers. However, there has been an increased concern in the business community that the informal and relatively easy contacts between business and government have been working less effectively.

After considering sources of a gap between actual manufacturing output and some socially optimal level of manufacturing output – and methods of narrowing any gap that exists – Albert Breton concludes: 'Other arguments brought forward to justify an industrial strategy must be assumed to be rationalization of some hidden special private interests. This danger is always present in government intervention, but it is not peculiar to an industrial strategy' (Breton, 1974, 24).

4
Industrial science policy as an aspect of nationalism

INTRODUCTION

Science policy has been defined by the Senate Special Committee as: 'the sum of legislative and executive measures taken to increase, organize and use the national scientific and technological potential with the object of achieving the country's overall development needs and enhancing its position in the world' (Report of Senate Special Committee, 1970, 2). Industrial science policy as a subset of a national science policy might, therefore, be considered as the sum of legislative and executive measures affecting the contribution of the application of scientific methods to the improvement of technology and management as used in industrial activities.

Such a definition of industrial science policy is clearly broad enough to admit a range of potential actions beyond the scope of analysis for this paper. Hence, in relating industrial science policy to a general model of economic nationalism, we shall concentrate on the generally expressed policy positions of public institutions with significant influence over policies affecting industrial innovation and technological diffusion. Where appropriate and important, specific measures derived from these policy positions will be introduced and considered.

A model of economic nationalism and a set of derived propositions, based on the work of Breton and Johnson, was presented in an earlier section. The general model posits that a primary objective of nationalism is to effect the transfer of property and jobs from non-nationals to nationals.[1] Derived propositions from

---

1 This transfer process is particularly emphasized in manufacturing industries possessing characteristics symbolic of industrial competence.

the general model of nationalism include: (a) a major effect of nationalism is to redistribute income from consumers and working class members to producers and middle class members; (b) its emergence will be correlated with the rise of new middle classes who have difficulty in finding suitable career opportunities.

Earlier chapters related commercial policy to the model of economic nationalism. The unique nature of Ontario's industrial structure, with its heavy emphasis on manufacturing industries, implies that the costs of a 'nationalist' bias in commercial policy will be particularly significant for that province. A similar inference can be drawn for a nationalist orientation towards science policies. Ontario is not only manufacturing intensive, but (as discussed in a later section) also concentrates a greater percentage of its manufacturing activity in 'high technology' industries as compared with other regions in Canada. Hence, science policy formulation, within the context of commercial policy, has particularly important implications for the growth and competitive ability of Ontario industries.

In the following section, we shall consider whether or not industrial science policy, as it has previously existed and is currently evolving, is consistent with policies derived from the general model of economic nationalism. An attempt will also be made to evaluate the potential consequences of such policies. The analysis will proceed by deriving propositions from the nationalism model relating specifically to science policy, and testing these propositions against observed government activities designed to promote the improvement of technology.

ELEMENTS OF A NATIONALIST SCIENCE POLICY

The broadest proposition would suggest that efforts to promote innovation and the diffusion of new technology be consistent with maximum ownership of property, including scientific and technical jobs, by members of the national group. More specifically, an industrial science policy consistent with economic nationalism would emphasize in deed, if not in word, the transference of technology-oriented job opportunities, both research and administrative, from non-nationals to nationals.

A corollary of this broad proposition is the hypothesis that Canadian scientific and technical workers, the suggested prime beneficiaries of science policies, have above average incomes, while inefficiencies resulting from the selected policies will impose costs primarily upon consumers and lower-income workers.

An examination of some general as well as several specific features of industrial science policy, as it is evolving at the federal level, lends support to assertions about the nationalist orientation of policy measures. Several specific elements of current science policy manifesting a nationalist orientation include: (a) opposition to foreign-owned subsidiaries, particularly in high-technology industries; (b) support for maintaining protective tariffs on consumer goods and on certain types of producer goods; (c) a preference for encouraging innovation over promoting the rapid adoption of existing best practice technology, particularly new technology developed by non-nationals.

Since actions and attitudes of science policymakers may be rationalized on grounds other than transferring jobs from non-nationals to nationals, we shall consider other possible motivations, as well as evaluate policies in the light of their expressed intentions.

GOVERNMENT FUNDING POLICIES

The most direct way that government can influence scientific activity, at least in the short run, is through research and development granting policies.[2] A prefer- for employing nationals in the technological-change effort is evident in specific government granting programs designed to increase productivity in Canadian manufacturing industries.[3] The major direct funding programs at the federal level are those administered by the Department of Industry, Trade and Commerce (ITC). The substantial incentive programs aimed at increasing industrial productivity include: IRDIA (the Industrial Research and Development Incentives Act), PAIT (Program for the Advancement of Industrial Technology), DIP (the Defence Industry Productivity Program), and IDAP (Industrial Design Assistance Program). In addition, there are a number of adjustment assistance programs including the Automotive Adjustment Assistance Program, the General Adjustment Assistance Program, and the Pharmaceutical Industry Development Assistance Program.

The major research and development incentive programs administered by ITC explicitly stress the requirement that new or improved technology be developed as much as possible in Canada. For example, IRDIA provides cash grants for current and capital expenditures for scientific research and development conducted in Canada (Department of Industry, 1970b). Eligibility under IDAP

2 Recent studies suggest that patterns of research and development funding are the most significant factor affecting income levels of scientific workers and employment levels of engineers. See R. Freeman, 'Supply and salary adjustment to the changing science manpower market,' *American Economic Review*, March 1975, and John F. O'Connell, 'The labor market for engineers: an alternative methodology,' *Journal of Human Resources*, Winter 1972.

3 Table 1 in Appendix A shows payments to Canadian industry for Research and Experimental Development, 1966-67 to 1971-72, by various government agencies.

requires that: 'the industrial design activity should be executed in Canada by designers resident in Canada. Foreign expertise may be used where Canadian expertise is not available' (Department of Industry, 1970*a*). Financial assistance under PAIT is available to Canadian incorporated companies for development projects to be carried out and exploited in Canada (Department of Industry, 1970*c*).

The major incentive programs encourage substitution of certain domestic resources for foreign resources by lowering the private costs of employing nationals in the technological change process.[4] A question raised is whether the same number of nationals would be hired even if no formal requirements existed in the programs. The fact that ratios of industrial scientists and engineers to total employees in Canadian manufacturing industries are positively related to government research and development funding is some evidence that federal granting programs do alter private costs of domestically developed versus foreign developed technology (Globerman, 1973).

It is not startling to find that government assistance programs directly emphasize the employment of nationals in the research and development process. Explicit statements attesting to the importance of creating favourable employment opportunities for nationals can also be found. For example, a report of the Science Council of Canada contains the following statement:

It should not be concluded that all those who have chosen training in science and technology should be entitled to employment in the field of their choice. The well-being of the nation requires that effective use be made of highly-trained people in all categories. However, public credibility will inevitably be strained if funds continue to be used to support and promote scientific education unless more effective use can be made of these graduates (Science Council of Canada, 1971, 19).

Nor is the emphasis on employment of nationals merely a recent feature of policy programs. Indeed, current science policy can best be understood in the context of an historic preference for promoting employment opportunities for domestic scientific and technical workers. The National Research Council, the formal institution initially instructed to coordinate and promote scientific and industrial research in Canada, stressed as one of its goals the avoidance of 'scientific colonialism' and the provision of ample job opportunities for

4 The Industrial Research Assistance Program initiated in 1962 and administered and financed by the National Research Council was designed to encourage longer-term applied research activities in Canadian industry. The IRA Program directly requires that companies add to their existing scientific and technical staffs in order to qualify for support. See Andrew H. Wilson, 1968, 132-3.

Canadian trained scientists (Report of Senate Special Committee, 1970, 86).

What is somewhat unique about current policy is the increasing preference for commercially oriented research and development to be performed directly by industry rather than by government laboratories. Previously, employment of high-level scientists and engineers was accomplished directly by hiring policies within government departments and agencies. Commercially useful results developed in government laboratories were presumably available to domestic industrial users. Policy emphasis is now coming to stress greater employment in industrial labs.[5] It is of interest to consider in more detail how specific policy orientations of science authorities are consistent with the nationalist orientation of past policies.

ATTITUDES TOWARDS FOREIGN OWNERSHIP

Current opposition to foreign-owned subsidiaries is a natural outgrowth of a preference for research and development to be performed by nationals. The multinational firm is an effective vehicle for the international specialization of labour including scientific and technical labour. It has also been suggested that it is a useful instrument for speeding diffusion of new technology to countries less well-endowed with managerial and scientific personnel. It seems a reasonable presumption that the real costs of transferring outside technology into domestic production processes will be lower for the subsidiary than for the domestically owned firm, other things being equal. Unit costs of information exchange may be lower for intra-firm than for inter-firm transfers. Economies of scale are also presumed to exist in the production of new technology. Certainly above-average levels of foreign ownership in technology-intensive industries constitute some evidence that multinational companies possess an advantage in the utilization of new technology.

The existence of economies of scale in the production and utilization of new technology encourages centralization of scientific and technological manpower

5 Table 2 in Appendix A illustrates the preference that Canada has, in the past, shown for research and development to be done by public agencies and universities as contrasted with an emphasis on industrial research and development manifested by other developed countries. The relative distribution of research and development expenditures shown might reflect not only public policy difference but also lower private rates of return to research and development expenditures in Canada than elsewhere. An earlier study pointed out some particular difficulties in estimating private rates of return to research and development expenditures in Canada, although private, intra-mural expenditures were found to have a statistically significant relationship to subsequent industrial growth. See S. Globerman, 1972.

in the parent company's head office. The subsidiary, in turn, generally 'rents' technical manpower services from the parent company. Domestically owned Canadian firms also tend to purchase outside technology, although purchases are primarily sourced through 'arms-length' licensing arrangements with foreign firms (Crookell, 1973). Such licensing operations frequently entail the use of manpower services provided by the licensor.

In-house technology personnel are ordinarily required to facilitate adoption of outside technology regardless of source. However, to the extent that economies of scale exist for technology transfers between parent and subsidiary, manpower requirements for any level of new technology adoption should be lower in the subsidiary than in a domestically owned firm licensing technology in the open market.[6]

To be sure, other objections have been raised against the presence of foreign-owned firms. It has been alleged that subsidiaries may be prevented from exploiting the full advantages afforded by new technology since such exploitation might result in decreased market shares of the parent firm. While a set of conditions can be described that, in the short run, would make it advantageous for the parent firm to impose restrictions on the use of new technology, it should be noted that restrictions may be imposed on the use of licensed technology for the same sets of reasons. Furthermore, there has, to date, been no persuasive evidence presented that foreign affiliation, per se, has an unfavourable effect upon export performance except in a small minority of cases (Safarian, 1966; Brash, 1966; Dunning, 1962; DIVO, 1969).

Opposition to foreign subsidiaries has also been founded on the notion that their presence contributes to an industrial structure that is not conducive to technological change. Policy-makers have pointed to high levels of foreign ownership as a major contributory factor to the 'fragmented' nature of most Canadian manufacturing industries. In considering barriers to successful innovation, the Science Council concludes: 'Our markets are fragmented by too many suppliers. This fragmentation is brought about by the widespread presence in Canada of branch plants and subsidiaries of foreign companies ... (Science Council of Canada, 1971, 28; Bourgault, 1973).

Evidence is accumulating that short production runs are a barrier to technological change in Canada.[7] Available studies, however, tend to conclude that foreign ownership is coincident with, rather than a cause of, the fragmented

6 Subsidiaries may also be less prone than domestically owned firms to hire domestic technical workers for nationally prestigious, but unprofitable, research and development undertakings.
7 This notion will be more completely developed in a later section.

structure of many secondary manufacturing industries. Short production runs in Canada are generally considered to be the result of the Canadian tariff (Daly, Keys, and Spence, 1968). In essence, the tariff permits both subsidiaries and domestically owned firms to produce an inefficiently wide range of output for any given plant size.

THE DOMESTIC TARIFF

Little explicit attention has been paid to the domestic tariff by science policy-makers. The tariff has been explicitly recognized as a potential impediment to technological change only insofar as it restricts imports of instruments and equipment used in industrial research and development (Meyboom, 1970). Hardly any recognition has been given to possible links between the domestic tariff, product lengths of run, and rates of technological change.

Several government programs designed to promote increased industrial efficiency recognize the potential impact of the tariff in reducing the inflow of new capital equipment embodying best practice technology. However, remissions of tariff duties are available only if such equipment is not domestically produced. The Automotive Adjustment Assistance Program administered by ITC allows up to 99 per cent of the duty on imported production machinery and equipment to be remitted if such machinery is not available from Canadian producers in time to meet production schedules. Similarly, the Machinery Program allows remission of duties on imported machinery equipment not available from Canadian production.

The existence of domestic tariffs across a wide range of secondary manufacturing goods has at least two potentially important indirect effects upon the domestic employment of scientific and technical workers. To the extent that new technology is embodied in capital equipment, the tariff – by raising the price of foreign produced capital goods – restricts the inflow of foreign technological services embodied in new equipment. The tariff also imposes differences between 'best practice technology' inside versus outside the domestic economy. Specifically, best practice technology developed outside the domestic economy tends to be embodied in indivisible units of capital.[8] To use such equipment economically often requires longer production lengths of run than are, in fact, typical of Canadian industrial structures characterized by excessive product diversity. As a result, importation of outside technology is reduced and/or additional services are required to 'scale down' the imported technology.

---

8 This is not an unrealistic assertion in that a substantial portion of new technology is developed in the United States and is appropriate to American production conditions.

In the next section, we shall present and attempt to support an argument that the existence of the domestic tariff both retards domestic rates of diffusion of new best practice technology and reduces the level of industrial innovation in Canada. Our argument rests largely on the notion that smaller plant sizes and excessive product diversity with consequent short production runs make it uneconomical for domestic producers to develop and/or adopt new techniques or products having large fixed cost components.

There is, indeed, a recognition among science policy-makers that small plant sizes and short production runs in Canadian secondary manufacturing industries create a climate in which large-scale research and development efforts are unprofitable. This recognition has led to some suggestions for encouraging mergers in order to create firms of sufficient size to undertake research and development projects (Provincial Bank of Canada, 1972). While tariff reductions would encourage increased specialization, from the standpoint of policy makers concerned with maximizing domestic employment of scientific and technical workers, merger policies are preferable to selective tariff reductions, since the additional costs imposed on imported technology embodied in foreign products would be maintained.[9]

INNOVATION VERSUS ADOPTION OF NEW TECHNOLOGY

Another element of nationalism evident in current science policy is the emphasis on innovation and originality in research and development undertakings. Government funding policies to promote technological change clearly exhibit this emphasis.[10] For example, the stated program principle of PAIT is to promote the growth and efficiency of industry in Canada by providing financial assistance for selected projects concerned with the development of new or improved products and processes which incorporate new technology (Department of Industry, 1970c, 2). Development is considered to entail improving a product or process by incorporating a significant technical advance, provided that the method followed is that of systematic investigation by means of experiment or analysis. If the

9 This point is clearly recognized in the following observation: 'Because of tariffs, new technology has not been imported into Canada embodied in products. Rather, it has come in the form of knowledge, skills and specifications' (Crookell and Wrigley, 1975, 60).

10 Past government funding policies as well as the nature of research and development performed directly by the government also bear this characteristic. Table 3 in Appendix A shows the significantly higher proportion of research and development expenditures devoted to fundamental and applied research in Canada as compared with other developed countries.

product or process is or has been substantially established, and the primary purpose is, among others, cost reduction, then the work is no longer development (Department of Industry, 1970c; Wilson, 1968).

Some of ITC's assistance programs seek indirectly to encourage more rapid adoption of existing technology. For example, an eligibility criterion of PEP (Program to Enhance Productivity) is that assisted projects involve only available technology, although the project must involve a significant departure from the company's traditional productivity improvement practices (Department of Industry, 1970d, 3). However, an emphasis on research is evident even in this program as companies are encouraged 'to undertake intensive studies of significant and imaginative efficiency-improvement projects' (Department of Industry, 1970d, 2).

One government program specifically designed to encourage technological diffusion is the Technical Information Service, established in 1945 to help small secondary manufacturing industries keep pace with advances in research and technology. Through a system of field offices, the Service provides information and advice on technological matters without cost. The program is a modest one, however, with limited industrial coverage. The Industrial Engineering Section has only nine engineers in the field. Their efforts are focused on small companies who are helped on a do-it-yourself basis (Canada Yearbook, 1973, 383).

Several arguments have been put forth supporting an emphasis on research and development to promote significant departures from existing technology. One suggests that 'creative' research and development provides the greatest growth-promoting impacts for the innovating firm, since successful innovation provides the innovator with a quasi-monopoly position in one or more product markets, allowing the existence of certain rents, including above average profits and sales.

The analogy at the aggregate level is based on the product life cycle hypothesis of trade. The hypothesis postulates the existence of a hierarchy of trade flows based upon the international pattern of innovation and imitation, over time. An implication of the product-cycle 'theory' is that industries in high wage countries must continuously innovate in order to maintain their comparative advantage vis-à-vis their counterparts in lower wage countries.

A growing number of empirical studies provide convincing evidence that inter-firm differences in technology are an important factor determining international trade flows for a variety of commodities (Vernon, 1970), as well as differential rates of growth in sales and profits across firms within domestic industries (Leonard, 1971). These aggregate studies cannot, however, provide evidence on whether dynamic comparative advantage deriving from changes in technology are created primarily by significant departures from prevailing technology, or by successful and rapid adoption of existing new technology.

While one can, to be sure, find individual cases of innovation having extremely high private (and social) rates of return, similar studies are available indicating that rates of return to successful adoption, which often included modest modifications of the original innovation, can also be quite high.

Enos divided technological progress in the petroleum refining industry into two phases, which he called alpha and beta. The alpha phase consisted of the invention, its succeeding development in both laboratory and pilot operations, and finally its installation or production in the first commercial plant. The beta phase comprised improvements on the innovation. Improvements could be of three types: the construction of larger units to take advantage of inherent economies of scale; the adoption of ancillary advances by other industries; and the increase in operating skill or knowhow (Enos, 1962, 317). Factor inputs and factor proportions for four different cracking processes were listed at the ends of the alpha and beta phases. Enos concludes that the beta phase was as significant in its economic effects as the alpha. There were greater reductions in factor inputs, per unit of output, when a process was improved than when it was supplanted by a better one (Enos, 1962, 319).

Tilton concluded that the market shares enjoyed by a handful of new semiconductor firms greatly surpassed their contributions to the innovative process. Firms achieved this result by being particularly adept in the diffusion process and leading in the use of new technology developed in their own and other laboratories to produce better and cheaper semiconductor devices (Tilton, 1971, 69).

Finally, a study of commercially successful technological advances found that a significant number (i.e., 23 to 33 per cent) were wholly adopted from other firms. These were more often process innovations than product innovations, and tended to be modifications rather than completely new items. The cost of adopted innovations was about the same as that of the original innovations, reflecting the fact that costs of originating and developing a successful innovation are a relatively minor part of the total cost of bringing it into use, i.e., about 5 to 10 per cent (Utterback, 1974, Appendix, Table 4).

In sum, the argument that economic growth is stimulated by significant innovation to a greater degree than from rapid adoption of existing best practice technology is unsupported by existing empirical studies.

A second argument put forth to support an emphasis on innovation is that indigenous and original research and development work provides experience for local research, technical, and managerial personnel. Adoption of outside technology, even when combined with adapting the technology to local specifications, is presumed not to provide the same sets of learning benefits.

Most observers of the technological change process would disagree that no learning benefits are associated with adopting existing 'best practice' technology.

As eminent an authority as Mansfield concludes that: 'The diffusion process, like the earlier stages of the process of creating and assimilating new processes and products, is essentially a learning process. However, rather than being confined to a research laboratory or to a few firms, the learning takes place among a considerable number of users and producers' (Mansfield, 1968, 112).

While both innovation and adoption may provide scientific and technical workers with employment and experience, it is likely that certain specific skills required to effect technology 'breakthroughs' are not required for adapting already existing technology to local production conditions, namely highly educated research personnel to perform both basic and applied research leading to the development stage. Unfortunately, available data do not allow testing of the hypothesis that average skill levels of research and technical workers in firms emphasizing innovation are higher than in firms emphasizing adoption of existing technology. Available studies do indicate, however, that skill-requirement ratios are fairly rigid in research intensive industries. That is, highly educated research personnel cannot readily be replaced by skilled technicians (Sargent, 1973; O'Connell, 1972).

PROVINCIAL SCIENCE POLICIES

Industrial development programs at the provincial level cannot be as clearly characterized by inferences drawn from a general model of nationalism. Development programs administered by agencies such as the Ontario Development Corporation and the Northern Ontario and Eastern Ontario Development corporations are not as specific as federal programs in requiring local content in capital purchases. Nor is there explicit insistence that new technology employed form unique additions to existing technical knowledge.

Capital costs, in principle, can be approved under the various programs for new machinery and equipment — regardless of source — as well as for new buildings, purchase of existing buildings, and the cost of their renovations and modification. Venture capital loans are available under the various programs to assist small Canadian-owned businesses in Ontario to introduce new technology. There is no explicit requirement that the new technology be developed and/or adapted by workers of national origin, nor must the new techniques adopted represent significant breakthroughs in technical knowledge.[11]

11 The stipulation that eligible small businesses be Canadian owned is, to an extent, redundant since multinationals tend to be concentrated in industries with above-average firm sizes.

The nationalist model has its application largely at federal levels of government.[12] Nationalism is a collectively consumed good and, like national defence, it is difficult to exclude non-payers from consumption. More specifically, efforts to alter factor prices of domestic versus foreign technical workers at the provincial level may be relatively ineffective because of the higher degree of interregional, as compared to international, mobility of labour. Quebec could constitute an important exception since mobility into and out of the provincial labour force might be more restricted (by language barriers, for example) than mobility among English-speaking workers across national borders. In effect, benefits of nationalist policies at a provincial level can be largely restricted to residents of Quebec.

REVIEW AND EXAMINATION OF PROPOSITIONS

Our limited examination to this point suggests that the objectives of the Canadian federal government and its actions to promote technological change are, and have been, consistent with the broad proposition derived from the general model of nationalism; that is, the federal government has placed a significant emphasis on the employment of national scientific and technical workers with less concern for allocative efficiency.

Additional evidence supporting this contention is provided by the observation that Canada has opted for a more labour-intensive research and development process than have most other countries. For example, of seven OECD countries, including the United States, France, Germany, Belgium, the United Kingdom, Sweden, and Canada, only Belgium devoted a smaller percentage of GNP to gross expenditures on research and development than did Canada in 1967. However, in terms of qualified scientists and engineers in research and development, as a percentage of the total labour force, Canada ranked below only the United States and France in 1967 (Report of the Senate Special Committee, 1970, 122). While it is unlikely that all countries possess identical production functions for research and development activity and that all face identical factor price ratios, it is equally unlikely that Canada's emphasis on skilled labour input purely reflects cost minimization along any research and development product 'isoquant.'

There is a substantial amount of evidence pointing to slower rates of technological change in Canadian manufacturing industries compared with the manufacturing industries of Canada's developed trading partners. The bulk of this

12 Breton's model of nationalism applied to Quebec is an exception.

evidence will be discussed in the following section. We will merely note here the results of a relatively recent OECD study that, employing four output perform- ance indicators of technological innovation, ranked Canada last in a sample of ten industrially advanced countries, although she ranked sixth in terms of total research and development expenditures, in millions of United States dollars, and sixth in total numbers of qualified scientists and engineers employed in research and development in 1967. (See Table 5 in Appendix A.) This result might be taken as some evidence that Canada is using her scientific and technical resources less efficiently than are other countries.

It should be noted that this inefficiency might reflect not only an un- economically high ratio of labour to capital in the research and development process, but also misallocations within the labour input category. Specifically, Canada has traditionally placed a larger percentage of her educational resources into training PhDs and supporting graduate research in science and engineering than has, for example, the United States.[13] Concomitantly, a much smaller per- centage of educational funds has been allocated to training industrial managers and administrators, in spite of recent studies of the innovation process which emphasize the crucial role of management activities, such as marketing, in suc- cessful innovation.

The corollary to the broad proposition is the hypothesis that science policy should promote a redistribution of income to beneficiaries; here Canadian scientists and engineers who already have above average incomes. Some limited and very imperfect data are available enabling us to examine the hypothesis. Table 6 in Appendix A provides evidence that employed scientific and technical workers had incomes in 1970 that were 60 to 70 per cent higher than incomes earned by all employed workers. It is evident that policies which promote income transfers from consumers, that is, all employed workers, to scientific workers would be income regressive.

The data in Table 6 cannot, of course, be taken as evidence that such trans- fers have taken place. Higher incomes of scientific workers could reflect a greater investment in human capital on the part of these workers. Some perspective on the wage-relative difference in Canada can be gathered by looking at comparable statistics for the United States. From data provided in the United States census, a category of scientific and technical workers, comparable with the category definition in the Canadian census, was developed. The American category was defined as employed persons, sixteen years and older, who were employed as

13 This is partly reflected in the observation that Canada has focused a greater percentage of her research efforts in higher educational institutions presumably emphasizing pure, as opposed to applied, research (see Table 2 in Appendix A).

either engineers, mathematics specialists, life scientists, physical scientists, or engineering and scientific technicians in 1969.

Data provided in Table 7 of Appendix A suggest that the structure of the labour market for scientific personnel in Canada does not contribute to higher relative earnings for these workers. While the relative supply of scientific workers is greater in the United States, relative earnings are also higher; however, this crude comparison is suspect in that other factors influencing income-relative differences are not held constant. One such factor is the relatively greater number of female scientific workers in Canada. The percentage of female to male scientific workers is 8.6 per cent in Canada versus 6.3 per cent in the United States. Another factor is the greater percentage of scientific and technical workers in manufacturing industries in the United States.[14] Earnings for scientific and technical workers in manufacturing are higher than the average for all other sectors.[15] Finally, scientific and technical workers in the United States have higher levels of formal education than do their Canadian counterparts (see Table 8 in Appendix A). The effects of added education on salaries in the scientific professions have been found to be quite substantial. For example, Freeman estimates that college-trained specialists in engineering earn 15 to 30 per cent more than non-degree engineers of the same age (Freeman, 1971, 28).

All of these factors cited would contribute to relatively higher earnings for scientific and technical personnel in the United States than in Canada. Unfortunately, data are not available allowing us to standardize for all worker quality differences, which would facilitate a 'clean' comparison of relative earnings in the two countries. At best, we are led to suggest that in light of major differences in factors affecting marginal productivities, the approximately 5 per cent relative earnings premium for American scientific and technical workers seems quite low. This small difference could reflect greater producer 'rents' being earned by Canadian scientific workers.

A full consideration of the distribution of costs associated with an inefficient allocation of scientific resources is beyond the scope of this study. Conceptually, the costs are associated with higher prices for goods and services produced in Canada and, to this extent, could be considered

14 Since census data on an industry basis are not available for Canada, this observation is made as an inference from Table 2 in Appendix A.
15 While the mean income of male science workers in the United States was approximately 38 per cent greater than the mean income of all employees, the mean income of male science workers in manufacturing industries was 45 per cent greater than the mean income of all manufacturing employees.

within the same analytical framework as the static costs of the tariff discussed in an earlier section.

It is noteworthy, as a derived proposition of the nationalist model, that the evolving emphasis on the employment of nationals in industrial research and development is coincident with expressed concerns about employment prospects for Canadian scientists and engineers. A Science Council Report suggested that only about one half of the 1972 output of scientific and engineering graduates would be effectively utilized in the near future. The overall imbalance between supply and demand could not be entirely attributed to current economic conditions since the potential surplus seemed greater for technical workers, especially for those with advanced degrees, than for non-technical graduates (Kelly, 1971, 13).

CONCLUSION

Our limited examination of the broad area of science policy suggests that government objectives and actions to promote technological change are, and have been, consistent with elements of a general model of economic nationalism: namely, in the emphasis placed on employment of national scientific and technical workers. This emphasis has been at the expense of greater efficiency in the allocation of scientific resources, in terms of the impact of science and technology on Canadian industrial growth.

To be sure, an argument exists that market allocation processes may lead to an underemployment of scientific personnel since many of the benefits of technological advances cannot be internalized as private returns to producers. We are not arguing in this section that government support of technological efforts, including basic research, leads per se to a misallocation of scientific resources. However, an efficiency argument supporting government subsidies to research and development activity does not imply that subsidies to scientific activity be restricted to efforts which employ only Canadian nationals or which are labour-intensive. As already indicated, such emphasis in science policy appears to give rise to allocative inefficiencies. If there are substantial external benefits to transferring employment opportunities from non-nationals to nationals, it needs to be demonstrated that these benefits exceed the welfare losses associated with resultant allocative inefficiencies.

5

The tariff and technological change

In this section, we consider the relationship between one specific and pervasive manifestation of nationalism – the tariff – and rates of innovation and diffusion in domestic industries. Our focus on the domestic tariff reflects not only the need to delimit research scope in an abbreviated paper but also our judgment that the tariff, through its impact upon industrial structure and levels of competition, is a major factor retarding more rapid rates of technological change in Canadian manufacturing industries.

Underlying our decision is a presumption that other important organizational characteristics of many Canadian manufacturing industries, or, at least, the impact of such characteristics on industrial performance, are related to the existence of the tariff. For example, high levels of industrial concentration, suggested as another factor contributing to industrial inefficiency in Canada (Economic Council of Canada, 1969, 79-81), may be a necessary but not a sufficient condition for the existence of production inefficiencies. In an open economy, increased imports – or even the possibility of market share loss through increased imports – should be an effective force restraining significant departures from allocative efficiency associated with imperfectly competitive domestic market structures.

The outline of a model relating domestic tariff levels to rates of technological change in domestic industries has been provided in some detail by other researchers, including those concerned with economic nationalism. It has been suggested that the tariff reduces rates of technological change in at least three distinct ways.

TARIFF-INDUCED CHANGES IN FACTOR PRICES

One way is by raising the cost of capital relative to labour in tariff-protected industries.[1] Salter (1966) has shown how this tendency will defer the date of obsolescence and result in a larger proportion of an industry's capital equipment being relatively outmoded. Furthermore, the 'best practice' plant in a protected country should be less capital-intensive than an equivalent plant in a free-trade country.[2] To the extent that technology is capital-embodied, the protectionist country will lag behind the free-trade country in the use of new production practices.

Available evidence indicates that the overall levels of capital per person employed are roughly equal in Canada and the United States, in spite of the differences in factor prices. The stocks of structures are higher in Canada in the three broad categories shown in Table 8 earlier, which may partly reflect the additional capital associated with extreme winter temperatures and greater seasonal variation. The rough comparability of equipment in manufacturing per person employed in the two countries merits further comment in light of its importance in this study, especially as machinery and equipment have been stressed in growth theories emphasizing capital-embodied technological change. The higher prices for machinery and equipment relative to labour in Canada that have persisted historically have been partially offset by faster write-offs for corporation tax purposes. As a result, the differences on an after-profits tax basis are less marked. In addition, in earlier interviews businessmen have pointed out that the costs of developing machinery for the different pattern of factor costs in Canada can frequently be more expensive than importing the machinery from the United States. It is also possible that the composition of industries within manufacturing is more capital-intensive than in the United States. These other factors apparently obscure or offset any effect of differences in factor prices in total manufacturing on the levels of machinery and equipment per person employed. The evidence is fairly clear that the levels of capital stocks in Canada

1 When American prices are used as a basis, average hourly earnings in Canadian manufacturing were approximately 81 per cent of earnings in American manufacturing for 1965, while machinery and equipment prices and long-term corporate bond prices were up to 26 per cent higher in Canada than in the United States. See D.J. Daly, B.A. Keys, and E.J. Spence, *Scale and Specialization in Canadian Manufacturing*, Staff Study No. 21 for the Economic Council of Canada (Ottawa: Queen's Printer, March 1968), p. 29. Chapter 3 above includes later data on the narrowing in weekly earnings for more recent years.

2 One can presume that not only will labour be substituted for capital in protected industries, but also (and perhaps to a greater degree) that fixed capital will be substituted for machinery and equipment.

are much higher than in most other countries, including the United States, both on a per person employed basis and as a share of non-residential fixed investment (Daly and Walters, 1967). On the other hand, the equipment share is below that in most other countries but still high on a per person employed basis compared to the European and developing countries. No direct evidence is available on age distributions of capital equipment in Canada and elsewhere, although available studies (which will be discussed subsequently) tend to show that Canadian firms, on average, adopt new machinery at a slower rate than do foreign firms.

THE TARIFF AND INDUSTRIAL STRUCTURE

Domestic tariff levels may also reduce rates of innovation and diffusion by fostering an industrial structure characterized by inefficiently small plant sizes producing a wide range of output for short production lengths of run. Evaluation of relationships between scale, specialization, and rates of technological change is made somewhat difficult by the various types of potential scale economies existing at the plant, firm, and industry levels.

At the root of any argument linking scale and specialization to rates of technological change is the notion that the development and/or adoption of new technology is characterized by significant fixed costs, and that innovation/ adoption can be profitable only if these costs are spread over large output volumes. To the extent that process innovations embodied in capital equipment are specific to a particular production process, the more relevant scale measure is production lengths of run within given plants. If the capital equipment can be transferred from one production process to another with little resulting downtime, the more appropriate scale consideration is total output volume at the plant level.

Product innovations are more clearly tied to production lengths of run within existing plants. Start-up expenses associated with prototype development in manufacturing are a significant component of the total costs of innovation, constituting between 10 to 25 per cent of all costs (U.S. Department of Commerce, 1967). Economies of scale at the firm level associated with marketing and financing activities should provide larger firms with an advantage in new product introduction. Marketing expenses are also a particularly important component of the costs of innovation, comprising a similar percentage of total costs as start-up expenses.

Static scale economies associated with spreading fixed costs of innovation and new technology adoption, both for new capital-embodied production processes and for new products, over larger output volumes are ordinarily reinforced by 'dynamic' scale economies associated with learning-by-doing. To the extent that learning economies are a function of accumulated output rates, costs of innovation and new technology adoption would be even more sharply decreasing functions of output.

Empirical evidence on the relationship between measures of firm size and innovation/diffusion processes is not entirely unambiguous, partly because of the difficulty in disentangling the various scale measures. Larger overall firm size is not consistently related to proportionately greater rates of innovation across all industries. For example, Mansfield found that the relative number of innovations carried out by the largest firms exceeded their relative share of the market for coal and petroleum firms but not for the largest steel producers (Mansfield, 1968a, 108-9). Tilton found that a significant percentage of new semiconductor devices were commercially introduced by small, relatively new firms (Tilton, 1971). This pattern has been observed as well for other branches of the electronic equipment and communications industries.

Part of the explanation for the finding that, in certain industries, smaller firms do proportionately more innovating than larger firms might be the fact that the smaller firms are highly specialized and, by concentrating on narrow product lines, are capable of achieving product lengths of run equal to those of larger but more diversified firms. Furthermore, learning economies associated with earlier production may be more important in these industries than are static economies associated with factor indivisibilities. The prototype small firm innovator in the semiconductor industry was usually highly specialized in a very limited number of semiconductor devices. The evidence with respect to technological diffusion as it relates to firm size is more clear cut. Empirical studies generally substantiate the hypothesis that large firms are quicker, on the average, than small firms to begin using new techniques.

THE TARIFF AND COMPETITIVE EFFICIENCY

A broader aspect of the relationship between tariffs and rates of technological change is the possibility that protective policies create monopolistic market conditions which seriously weaken the pressures and incentives for improved efficiency. Available empirical evidence is quite consistent in suggesting that high levels of industrial concentration along with other barriers to effective competition seriously reduce rates of adoption of new technology (Romeo, 1975). A more general study of efficiency in twenty-six Swedish manufacturing industries concluded that domestic tariffs adversely and significantly affected plant-level production efficiency (Carlsson, 1972).

Relatively little empirical work has been done in Canada on patterns of industrial innovation and diffusion and even less by way of attempts to explain observed patterns. Comparisons of domestic patents filed by residents as a percentage of all patents filed as well as of payments for technical services as a percentage of domestic research and development expenditures across developed countries indicate that Canadian industries are particularly large importers of foreign technology and lag behind in rates of industrial innovation (Firestone, 1971). Trade studies demonstrating that Canada's comparative disadvantage in secondary manufacturing is particularly marked for 'technology intensive' industries provide additional evidence that Canadian manufacturing industries suffer slower rates of technological change than their foreign counterparts (Weiser and Jay, 1972; Baumann, 1974). Limited information from case studies also suggests that Canadian firms are slower adopters of new technology developed outside the country. For example, Hufbauer, in a study on the diffusion of synthetic materials, found that production of a new synthetic first took place in Canada approximately fourteen years, on the average, after it had been initially produced by the innovating country (Hufbauer, 1966, 138).

Previous studies cited have, by and large, failed to treat explicitly the linkages between scale, specialization, and other derived consequences of the domestic tariff and subsequent rates of technological change in Canada. In the following sections, two sets of studies are discussed which attempt to provide additional evidence on rates of technological change in Canadian manufacturing industries as well as some explanation of observed rates. The first set consists of case studies of adoption patterns for several specific innovations. The second is an empirical investigation of the determinants of relative trade balances for a sample of secondary manufacturing industries.

NUMERICAL CONTROL MACHINE TOOLS

The first innovation we consider is the use of numerical control machine tools. The term 'numerical control' has come to be accepted as the control of a specific operation by means of tape or card command or by dial input. Numerical control, henceforth NC, has to date been applied chiefly to metal-working tools and, within this activity, chiefly to drilling, boring, and milling operations. NC machine tools are built in a wide variety of types and sizes ranging from relatively low-priced, multipurpose drilling machines to large machining centres capable of performing a wide variety of operations with automatic tool changers.

Consistent time series data on the adoption pattern for NC machine tools within a specific industry, the tool and die industry, are available for the United States.

TABLE 15

Per cent of tool and die firms in
U.S. using NC

Year (January 1)	Per cent of firms
1961	1.1
1962	1.1
1963	2.3
1964	4.5
1965	5.7
1966	7.9
1967	13.6
1968	20.4

TABLE 16

Per cent of tool and die firms in
Canada using NC

Year end	Per cent of firms
1961	1.54
1962	1.43
1963	1.33
1964	2.54
1965	4.76
1966	4.60
1967	4.49
1968	10.11
1969	11.11
1970	14.44
1971	16.67
1972	18.89

The percentage of American tool and die firms using NC over the period 1960-68 is given in Table 15 (Mansfield, 1968b). In order to facilitate direct comparison with the American study, comparable data were collected for the Canadian tool and die industry (Globerman, 1975b). The percentage of tool and die firms in Canading using NC over the period 1961-72 is given in Table 16.

Comparison of Tables 15 and 16 show that while initial adoption levels in the two industries were roughly equal, NC use spread more rapidly in the American industry than in Canadian; by 1968, roughly 20 per cent of the industry was using NC in the United States while in Canada the adoption level was closer to 10 per cent.

More specific comparisons of rates of diffusion were obtained by estimating parameters of a logistic function fit to the data in Table 16. The equation of the logistic function is given as:

$$P(t) = K/1 + e - (\propto + \phi t), \tag{1}$$

where $P(t)$ is the proportion of tool and die firms using NC at time t, K is the maximum proportion of user firms that will be reached, and $\propto$ and ϕ are the parameters of the logistic function.

Two values of K were assumed, 50 per cent and 80 per cent. These values were suggested by Mansfield based on interviews he conducted with a number of American tool and die firms. The parameters of the equation were estimated by taking natural logs of both sides of the equation, rearranging terms, and using ordinary least squares. Results are given below:[3]

$$\ln (Pt/0.50 - Pt) = -1.774 + 0.1333t \tag{1a}$$
$$\bar{R}^2 = 0.961 \qquad (14.61),$$

$$\ln (Pt/0.80 - Pt) = -1.961 + 0.1257t \tag{1b}$$
$$\bar{R}^2 = 0.948 \qquad (14.21),$$

The equations are estimates for the full period 1961-72. For comparison, estimates of the parameters of the logistic obtained by Mansfield from data in Table 15 are given below:

$$\ln (Pt/0.50 - Pt) = -4.604 + 0.538t, \tag{1c}$$

$$\ln (Pt/0.80 - Pt) = -4.460 + 0.466t. \tag{1d}$$

Comparison of equations (1a) through (1d) indicates that over a very similar time period, and for the same initial level of NC use, the rate of diffusion was approximately four times greater in the United States than in Canada. More significantly, this conclusion is maintained even if the 'optimistic' value of K, 80 per cent, is assumed for American firms and the 'pessimistic' value of K, 50 per cent, is assumed for Canadian firms.

When the sample was split into those firms using NC by the end of 1972 and those not using NC, we found NC users to be significantly larger than non-

---

3 A t value is shown in parentheses below the slope coefficients. $\bar{R}^2$ is the coefficient of determination adjusted for degrees of freedom.

users, as measured by total number of employees. In addition, users engage in significantly more precision machining activities, for which NC is particularly suited.

The results are consistent with the characteristics of the NC innovation. Since NC machines are ordinarily more expensive than the machines replaced, the overall volume of work to be done on NC equipment should be sufficient to keep the machine relatively busy and help spread overhead costs. Thus, one would expect NC to be more profitable for larger firms, other factors being the same. Furthermore, effective use of NC requires a company to preplan the manufacture of parts, operation by operation. The likelihood is greater that large, rather than small, firms engage, or have the capacity to engage, in production control activities necessary for successful NC use. Moreover, the advantages of NC are particularly suited for operations when the part configuration is complex and when parts involve many complicated operations, both of which are characteristics of precision machining activities.

While NC machine tools are capable of performing a variety of operations, the advantages gained by a larger overall work volume may be offset if production runs for particular operations are very small. This condition would arise if increased work volume was concomitant with proportionally increased product diversity. Among other factors, the relative advantage of NC machines depends upon average batch size and how often production of the same piece is repeated. The lot-sizes for which NC is most economic vary from workpiece to workpiece and from machine to machine; however, the technique has generally been found to be most favourable within the range of five to fifty pieces (Gebhardt and Hertzold, 1974). NC use would be clearly uneconomical for tooling processes involving one-off runs of a relatively unsophisticated part.

We were unable to obtain estimates of average lot-sizes for our sample of tool and die firms. It is likely, however, that firms enjoying larger overall work volumes also realized larger lot-sizes for any machining operation, since there are a relatively limited number of parts produced and tooling operations performed in a custom machine shop. Unfortunately, a measure of overall plant size does not allow us to separate the effects of length of run from other possible firm level economies since, in this industry, virtually all shops were single plant enterprises.

Some indirect evidence that average lot sizes are an important factor in the NC adoption decision of Canadian firms is provided by the following result: all non-user firms in our survey were asked to rank reasons for non-use on a scale ranging from unimportant to very important. Approximately 70 per cent of non-NC users cited too-short production runs as a very important reason for non-adoption. Two other reasons cited as very important, although by less than 30 per cent of non-NC users, were unfamiliarity with NC and inability to finance investment in NC. This may be taken as some indication that production lengths of run are the major scale factor associated with the NC adoption decision.

The tool and die industry, composed largely of independent machine shops and departments within integrated firms, is primarily a localized industry. It is, therefore, somewhat of a presumption to ascribe the smaller plants and smaller average batch sizes in Canada, as compared with the United States, to the existence of the Canadian tariff on machine tooled parts.[4] Nevertheless, the industry does receive significant tariff protection. The ratio of 1969 import duties paid to total imports for the machine shop sector in the metal fabricating group was 5.5 per cent while the comparable ratio for the counterpart American industry was about one per cent.

SPECIAL PRESSES IN PAPER-MAKING

The second innovation considered is the use of special presses in the paper process. The purpose of special presses, henceforth SPs, is to speed up the removal of water from the paper web, the substance of which paper is made, consisting of fibres and water, in the wet-end of the paper machine. The primary advantages of SPs over conventional suction presses are the significant increases in water removal, with resultant speed and production increases, along with reduced crushing and marking of sheets. SPs are suitable for all kinds of paper machines and are adaptable to existing presses with some modification.

The Venta-nip press, the most commonly used type of special press, was first adopted in the United States in 1963 and in Europe in early 1964. Two measures of the subsequent diffusion of SP use in Europe are available: the percentage of firms over time using SP-equipped machines, and the share of total output over time produced on SP-equipped machines[5] (see Tables 17 and 18).

4 The median number of employees at the beginning of 1968 for the sample of American tool and die firms was 36 while the median for our Canadian sample in 1972 was approximately 22.
5 The data indicate that the percentage of firms using SP-equipped machines is larger than the percentage of total output produced on SP-equipped machines. This relationship is a fundamental feature of diffusion patterns. Earlier adopters do not adopt as intensively as later adopters, other factors being equal, since the risks of adoption decrease over time. A complete description of the survey from which these data are derived is in Ray, 1969.

TABLE 17

Per cent of European firms using
SP-equipped machines

	1964	1966	1968
Austria		60	
Germany		33	75
Italy		22	55.5
Sweden	7.3	44	51.2
U.K.	4.3	21.3	63.8

TABLE 18

Per cent of total output produced on SP-equipped
machines, Europe (selected years)

	1964	1966	1968
Austria		42	52
Germany		4	23
Italy		6	
Sweden	2	24	52
U.K.	2	10	31

To obtain data on SP use in Canada, one of the authors conducted a mail survey of firms in the Canadian paper and board industry (Globerman, in press). Our survey indicated that the first use of SPs in Canada took place in 1963. Subsequent diffusion of SP use in Canada was measured as the percentage of responding firms over time indicating SP use, and the percentage of total industry output produced on SP-equipped machines. These data are shown in Table 19.

In comparing diffusion rates among the sample countries, it should be borne in mind that survey coverage varied considerably from country to country. While there was some over-representation of larger firms, who were earlier users of SPs, in both studies, this bias was particularly severe for several of the European countries. It is unlikely, however, that any adjustments for this bias would alter the fundamental conclusion that the inter-firm diffusion rate was slower in Canada than in Western Europe.

The characteristics of SP user and non-user firms in Canada were examined. It was expected that differences among firms in their SP-adoption behaviour would largely reflect differences in the relative advantage to each firm of using SPs. The most important advantage of SP use is considered to be the resulting increase in capacity of SP-equipped machines.

TABLE 19

Per cent of firms in Canada
using SP-equipped machines

1966	1968	1972
17.4	47.8	70.8

Per cent of total output
produced on SP-equipped
machines (selected years)

1965	1972
2.1	39.8

The potential advantage of increased capacity would be more completely realized, other things being equal, by firms producing standardized products, thus avoiding machine down-time associated with frequent product changeover, as well as by firms facing highly elastic demand curves for their products.[6] Previous researchers have noted that in the tariff-protected, that is, non-newsprint sector of the paper industry, the number of firms producing any product line has been too great for any one firm to achieve the lengths of run possible on modern paper-making machines (Haviland, Takacsy, and Cape, 1968). A related notion is that significant increases in sales of non-newsprint products by any one producer would require price reductions and, consequently, invite the possibility of retaliation by other producers. Given this situation, domestic producers will opt for stable shares of a smaller overall market.

An attempt was made to identify important differences among earlier and later SP-adopting paper companies. It was not possible to estimate directly the extent of product variation (associated with domestic tariff protection) for firms in our sample; however, an indirect measure of tariff protection, that is, the proportion that non-newsprint production comprised of total firm output, was found to be negatively and significantly related to the initial date of SP-adoption for our sample of paper companies.[7] Other factors being constant, larger firms did not adopt sooner than smaller firms. Older equipment in place contributed

6 Other things being constant, resultant increases in potential capacity will be smaller the older the machine being re-equipped.
7 Another measure of product variation was the calculated production volume per machine, taken to be a direct measure of the intensity of machine utilization. Since the two variables had a simple correlation coefficient of above 0.8, results were insensitive to our product variation measure.

to later SP-adoption, although the coefficient for the age of equipment variable was statistically insignificant at any acceptable confidence level. Finally, foreign-owned firms (those companies having more than 50 per cent of their assets owned by non-residents) were significantly earlier adopters than domestically owned firms.

Results cited above were concerned with how quickly firms began to use SPs. Another consideration is how quickly, once the innovation was adopted, its use spread within the firm. A measure of the rate of intra-firm adoption chosen for our sample was the number of years beyond the initial date of SP adoption it took for a firm's total output to be produced on SP-equipped machines.[8]

The most important variables influencing the intra-firm rate of adoption were the date of first adoption itself and the proportion of total output composed of non-newsprint products. Since the risk of innovation adoption can be expected to decrease over time as more experience with the innovation is accumulated outside the firm, the later the year of first adoption the quicker, other factors being equal, should be the intra-firm diffusion rate. This hypothesis was supported by our empirical results. The findings that firms enjoying greater tariff protection were slower to intensify SP use once the innovation was adopted are consistent with results from the inter-firm diffusion analysis.[9]

RELATED STUDIES

Diffusion patterns for NC machine tools and for special presses are specific examples of the possible impact that limitations on realized scale and specialization might have on adoption of — more or less — indivisible capital equipment. A recently completed study of innovation/diffusion patterns for a sample of Australian manufacturing industries provides some additional evidence on rates of innovation adoption in Canada as well as on the relationship between scale and specialization and adoption of capital-embodied new technology (Australian Government Publishing Service, 1972).

The study focused on ten industries and involved comparison of Australian experience with that of six other industrial nations including Canada. For at

8 Over half of our sample companies were producing all of their output on SP-equipped machines by the end of 1972. The date of total adoption for firms not yet at that level by the end of 1972 was estimated by extrapolating the annual rate of adoption up to 1972.

9 Our results also indicated that ownership is a far less important factor influencing the rate at which the innovation spread within a firm than in influencing the initial date of adoption. Moreover, larger firm size contributed to delays in intensifying the use of SPs within paper companies.

least two innovations in each industry, the authors attempted to identify two stages in the adoption process: the date of first adoption and the dates at which the innovations could be considered as having been 'generally accepted.'[10]

A general observation consistent with evidence in the study is that both Canada and Australia tended to have later initial adoption dates and later dates of 'general acceptance' than did other sample countries, primarily for innovations involving large capital expenditures. This observation leads the authors of the Australian study to conclude that encouraging rationalization through increasing production lengths of run and average plant size would improve diffusion of new technology.

It is also interesting to note an observation that parallels an earlier point raised in our study, namely, that various government incentive programs do little to encourage explicitly more rapid adoption of existing technology developed abroad. Indeed, through the maintenance of protective tariffs, this process for transferring technology is actually discouraged. In considering Australian government policy, the authors comment:

Adoption of new technology often tends to take place during actual production, after the new process or machine is installed. The incentive for increased R&D expenditure provided by the Industrial Research and Development Grants Act, 1967, does not provide industry with significant assistance when imported technology is adopted in this way. This is particularly true for the more fragmented industries containing many smaller sized companies (Australian Government Publishing Service, 1972, 1.5).

The evidence presented, to this point, is consistent with the hypothesis that the domestic tariff retards the diffusion of new technology in Canada by reducing the profitability of adopting capital-embodied innovations. A related hypothesis is that the tariff – by reducing competitive pressures to moderate costs – enables Canadian producers to indulge in excessive risk avoidance and eschew investment in risky, albeit profitable, new technology, even when the new technology is less capital intensive than existing production techniques. The diffusion pattern of a new production technique in the carpet industry provides further evidence on the potential significance of the latter relationship.

---

10 A major shortcoming of the study is the fact that data on actual adoption levels over time were not obtained. Rather, information on dates of first adoption and dates of acceptance were obtained from interviews with suppliers and users of the innovation. Hence, dates are relatively imprecise and – in many instances – little more than rankings of countries are provided.

TUFTING EQUIPMENT IN CARPET MAKING

A major post-war innovation in the carpet industry was the use of tufting machinery. Prior to the introduction of the tufting process, weaving was the principal method of carpet-making. The major advantage of the tufting process was that tufted carpets could be produced about one-third cheaper than traditional woven carpets. Early weaknesses of tufting, primarily the inability to make patterned carpets, were largely overcome by progress made in carpet printing technology.

The earliest use of tufting equipment in the United States took place around 1950 (Globerman, 1975). In 1952, it was estimated that about 14 per cent of the total broadloom carpet produced in that country was of tufted construction, and, by 1955, American tufted production amounted to about 40 per cent of total carpet production. This ratio increased to more than 60 per cent by 1957 and to 87 per cent by 1963.

By comparison, the first recorded use of the tufting process in Canada was in 1953; tufted carpet production as a percentage of total carpet output in that year can only be estimated as something less than 15 per cent. By 1960, tufted carpets constituted about 59 per cent of the total square yards of carpet produced in Canada, the ratio increasing to a peak of 80 per cent by the end of 1969.

In sum, a three-year lag existed between the initial production of tufted carpet in the United States and in Canada, although as late as 1953, the adoption level in the former was only 14 per cent, presumed to be not much higher than in Canada. It took approximately five years, 1952-57, from an initial level of 14 per cent, for tufted carpet output in the United States to reach 60 per cent of total carpet output. Starting from a roughly similar adoption level, it took about seven years, 1953-60, to achieve the 60 per cent adoption ratio in Canada. Moreover by 1960, 74 per cent of all carpet output produced in the United States was of tufted construction.

The major factor encouraging rapid adoption of tufting technology in the United States was the entry of new firms into the industry in the early post-war period. The number of firms manufacturing carpet doubled between 1949 and 1963, and all the new firms were users of the tufting process. The entrance of new tufting firms, in turn, compelled adoption of the tufting process by the relatively large, established carpet manufacturers (Reynolds, 1968).

Conditions in the United States were conducive to the entry of new firms into the industry in the early post-war period. Reynolds notes that no significant barriers to entry existed in the industry. Product differentiation was limited and the demand for carpets was price-elastic. The tufting process, in fact, had *lower* capital requirements than the conventional weaving process as smaller plant sizes were required. Barriers to entry for new carpet firms were significantly higher in Canada over a similar time period. The Canadian carpet industry was characterized by a greater degree of product differentiation because of the far fewer numbers of manufacturers, relative to total domestic output, operating in Canada.

One indication of the difference between competitive conditions existing in American and Canadian carpet industries is industry concentration ratios. The value of industry production accounted for by the eight largest firms in the American carpet industry in 1947 amounted to 71.2 per cent. In comparison, the number of firms accounting for 80 per cent of total employment in the carpet, mat, and rug industry in Canada during 1948 was 4.8. Another measure of differences in internal barriers to entry is price elasticities of demand in the two countries. Reynolds estimated the price elasticity of demand for carpets in the United States to be approximately equal to 1.35 over the period 1951-63. Using similar data, our estimated price elasticity of demand for carpets in Canada, over the period 1949-64, was 0.67.

The carpet industry in Canada during the post-war period can be aptly described by the model of a protected oligopoly, developed by Eastman and Stykolt (1967). High domestic levels of concentration along with effective product differentiation prevented entry of new tufters in the early diffusion period.[11] In this circumstance, increased imports might have served the same function as entry of new firms into the domestic industry by way of encouraging established firms to adopt tufting more quickly than they did. However, imports as a percentage of total factory shipments in Canada increased from a ratio of 0.57 in 1950 to a high of only 0.67 in 1954. Protective tariff levels along with the inelastic price demand for carpets and relatively high transport costs apparently prevented major import incursions into domestic markets.[12] Thus, later adoption of the tufting process by firms in Canada did not result in major loss of market shares to foreign exporters.

SUMMARY AND CONCLUSIONS OF CASE STUDIES

The evidence from the various case studies cited is consistent in demonstrating slower adoption of capital-embodied innovations in Canada than in several other developed countries. In cases where the innovation was more capital intensive

11 Barriers to domestic entry decreased over time as income increased and potential
   demand at existing prices increased.
12 The carpet, mat, and rug industry has nominal tariff rates significantly above the average
   for all manufacturing industries, equal to about 25 per cent in 1969.

than existing techniques, thus requiring longer product lengths of run for efficient use, slower adoption reflected the impact of the domestic tariff on plant level production conditions. The experience of the carpet industry suggests that the anti-competitive effects of the tariff might retard the adoption of new techniques even when the innovations are less capital intensive than existing techniques.

A potential concern is the need to reconcile Canada's slower rate of diffusion with the evidence on narrowing differences in output per capita between Canada and the United States. Table 4 above shows that there actually has been very little narrowing in output per employed person in manufacturing. The possibility of an aggregation bias must be recognized, although, given the number of factors affecting productivity, one can imagine that slower diffusion rates have been offset by other factors. Another possibility is that concomitant with Kennedy Round tariff reductions, the rate of diffusion has increased in Canada over time. A study by Hufbauer offers some tentative support for this hypothesis. In a study of the diffusion of synthetic materials, he found that production of a new synthetic first took place in Canada approximately fourteen years, on the average, after it had been initially produced by the innovating country. The most recent estimate of the lag was for 1962. By way of comparison, the lag between initial production of new synthetics in Canada and the innovating country was, on average, calculated as thirty-two years in 1910 (Hufbauer, 1966, 138). To evaluate in detail the hypothesis that diffusion rates in Canada have changed systematically over time is somewhat beyond the scope of this study.

The evidence with respect to the influence of foreign ownership is, at best, indecisive. In one case, an affiliate status increased the probability of early innovation adoption, while, in other cases, it had no significant influence on adoption behaviour. One should not be dismayed to find that diffusion gaps in Canada persist in spite of high foreign ownership levels. The result is consistent with other findings that, given existing tariff levels, subsidiaries do not act in any fundamentally different way from domestically owned firms (Safarian, 1966).

TRADE-FLOW STUDIES

Limitations on the inferences one can draw from a few, very specific case studies are recognized. The innovations investigated were all capital-embodied process innovations, while, in fact, the most common form taken by new technology (and to which the bulk of industrial research and development efforts are directed) is product development and modification.

In this section, a more general treatment is given to the relationship between industrial structure and technological change (presumed to include new product development). The analysis proceeds by calculating a measure of relative net trade balance for a sample of Canadian secondary manufacturing industries and relating our calculated measure to various industry characteristics including nominal domestic tariff rates. Several existing empirical studies of international trade flows, based upon 'technology-gap' trade theories, have noted the significant comparative disadvantage that Canada suffers in technology-intensive industries. Our intention here is to consider whether Canada's technology 'gap' is derived from some unique factor supply problem or whether it can be explained primarily by market structure factors and, in particular, by the existence of domestic and foreign tariffs.

The sample size was limited to fifty-four three- and four-digit Canadian secondary manufacturing industries for both pragmatic and conceptual considerations. Specifically, primary manufacturing industries were excluded since the factors influencing export-import flows have been found to differ significantly between primary and secondary manufacturing industries (Fullerton and Hampson, 1957). Of the total sample of secondary manufacturing industries, bakeries, breweries, distilleries, soft drinks, lime, cement and concrete products, and printing and publishing were excluded because of the primarily localized nature of production and sales in these industries. The manufacturing industries remaining in our sample are those for which information could be obtained on all variables of interest.

Our measure of relative trade balance is derived from a measure used by Balassa in an earlier study. Balassa measured a country's comparative advantage by dividing the country's share in the export of a given commodity by its share in the combined exports of manufactured goods of the ten industrial countries in his sample and expressing this result in index number form (Balassa, 1965).

Our measure, for the fifty-four secondary manufacturing industries, is calculated by dividing the dollar value of exports minus imports averaged over 1969-70 for each industry by the dollar value of exports minus imports over the same period for all industries in the sample. Net trade balance of each industry is standardized for industry size by dividing the calculated trade balance by the total value of industry shipments averaged for 1969-70; likewise, the aggregate net trade balance figure is divided by total value of shipments for all industries in the sample. Thus, our measure of relative trade balance, henceforth r.t.b., can be expressed as follows:

$$(\text{r.t.b.})i = \left. \left[(x_i - m_i) \middle/ v_i \right] \middle/ \left[(x_t - m_t) \middle/ v_t \right] \right.,$$

where x_i is the exports of the ith industry; m_i is imports of the ith industry; v_i is value of shipments of the ith industry; x_t is total exports of our fifty-four industries; m_t is total imports; and v_t is total value of shipments for the sample. All variables are average values for 1969-70.[13]

The net trade balance measure was chosen as a convenient summary measure of trade performance by industry; however, as mentioned above, such a measure might obscure certain behavioural relationships since determinants of export and import patterns may differ. More specifically, there is a concern that the net trade balance measure might be substantially influenced by erratic foreign and domestic tariffs, thereby distorting conclusions drawn about underlying comparative advantage. To some extent, the distortions created by the American tariff would be compensatory to those created by the domestic tariff, since tariff structures are similar (although lower in the United States). Thus exports from high tariff industries in Canada would be discouraged by the American tariff, while imports from the United States would be reduced by the domestic tariff. Interpretation of the statistic as an index of comparative advantage might thereby remain unaffected. Indeed, Balassa found a considerable degree of correspondence between export performance and export-import ratios for his sample of countries with Canada showing the highest correlation coefficient between the two sets of indices (Balassa, 1975, 108-9).

Our calculated measure of r.t.b. for each sample industry is given in Table 20.[14]

Since there was an overall net trade deficit, on average, for our sample of secondary manufacturing industries, calculated r.t.b.s were multiplied by minus one so that a positive value would reflect a net trade surplus in an industry. Industries for which the calculated statistic is positive can be considered as sectors in which Canada has a comparative advantage. Industries for which the statistic has a calculated value of less than minus one are the least internationally

13 Value of shipment data were obtained from Statistics Canada (1969, 1970) and export-import data are from Barrows (1973).
14 The full list of industries is given in Appendix B. For convenience, the industries are referred to by their SIC codes in the text. To evaluate the consistency involved in using alternative trade performance indices, an index of relative export performances was calculated for each industry. The measure was calculated by dividing the ratio of exports to total industry shipments, 1969-70, for the ith industry by the same ratio averaged for all industries in the sample. Industries were grouped by the three categories given in Table 15, and an average export intensity measure was calculated for the three industry sets. The average export intensity ratio calculated for the set of industries given under the first r.t.b. column in Table 20 was 1.99 while calculated ratios for the second and third column industries were 0.86 and 0.73 respectively. Our export performance measure, while providing the same grouped industry rankings as the net trade balance measure, is less precise in distinguishing categories of 'comparative disadvantage' industries.

TABLE 20

Relative trade balance, Canada, 1969-70

r.t.b. > 0		−1 < r.t.b. < 0		r.t.b. < −1	
Industries	r.t.b.	Industries	r.t.b.	Industries	r.t.b.
151	1.80	153	−0.03	1094	−3.40
		162	−0.95		
252	0.68	165	−0.65	172	−1.90
		183	−0.69		
2541	0.15	231	−0.22	174	−1.02
		248	−0.05		
256	0.56	2619	−0.11	175	−1.19
		266	−0.18		
264	0.24	272	−0.62	181	−1.25
		291	−0.06		
323	1.54	292	−0.40	182	−2.86
		3039	−0.24		
325	1.44	305	−0.99	268	−5.66
		311	−0.96		
327	0.05	324	−0.55	294	−1.31
		326	−0.01		
335	0.09	3391	−0.83	306	−3.39
		377	−0.26		
338	0.50	3991	−0.51	316	1.69
		374	−0.63		
		3651	−0.37	331	−1.88
		332	−0.95		
		321	−0.43	393	−3.09
		307	−0.17		
		301	−0.01	373	−1.92
		378	−0.63		
		375	−0.31	336	−1.54
		376	−0.14		
				334	−1.94
		304	−0.24		

competitive secondary manufacturing industries in the sample, while those industries having negative r.t.b.s greater than minus one and less than zero fall in between.

The first relationship we examined was that between the technological intensity of an industry, measured as the ratio of male professional and technical wage earners to total employees in the industry for 1961, and the industry's r.t.b.[15] While a more specific measure, such as the number of scientists and engineers as a percentage of total employees, might have been preferable to the measure chosen, data are not available at sufficiently disaggregated levels to estimate such a skill-specific human-capital ratio. Some consolation can be drawn from the fact that, at the two-digit level, ratios of professional and technical workers to total employees and R + D as a percentage of sales are highly correlated (Wilkinson, 1966, 13).

Mean ratios of professional and technical workers to total employees were calculated for our three sets of industries (see Table 21.) The mean ratio for the first industry category, those industries with r.t.b. indexes greater than zero, was 4.5 per cent, while for the other two sets the ratio was 6.4 per cent. It would appear that, while Canada has a comparative disadvantage in technology-based industries, the relationship between net-trade deficit and technological intensity may be non-linear and, perhaps, not monotonically increasing.

The limitations on inferences drawn from a crude statistical approach, such as employed above, are recognized. One major limitation of the above, as well as of all subsequent calculations, is the small number of observations in the comparative-advantage industry category. Another is the failure to explicitly incorporate ceteris paribus assumptions through statistical techniques such as multiple regression analysis; however, even if regression techniques were employed, unique parameter estimates would be difficult to obtain given, as will be shown, the intercorrelation existing among industry variables.

The mean domestic tariff level for the three sets of industries was found to increase consistently across categories.[16] The ratio of import duties to total imports in 1969 averaged 10.3 per cent for the first set, those industries with r.t.b.s greater than zero, while the average increased to 15.6 per cent for the second set, those with r.t.b.s between zero and minus one, and 17.1 per cent for the third, those with r.t.b. indices less than minus one. Relative net trade deficits are therefore seen to be consistently related to nominal domestic tariff levels. This result coincides with Baumann's findings (Baumann, 1974b) for sixty-seven three-digit Canadian industries that exports minus imports as a percentage of domestic output was inversely related to the Canadian tariff.[17] It is interesting to note that among those industries suffering comparative disadvantages, nominal tariff levels appear to exert an independent influence on the magnitude of trade

15 Information from the 1971 census was not available at the time the data were prepared and the data have not been recalculated when revising for publication.
16 Nominal tariff rates for our sample industries are provided in Lermer, 1974.
17 Baumann also points out the important disclaimer that the direction of causation is difficult to determine since high tariffs may also be the result of chronic trade deficits.

TABLE 21

Mean values of variables r.t.b. indices, Canada, 1969-70

	r.t.b. > 0	−1 < r.t.b. < 0	r.t.b. < −1
1 Professional and technical workers as a percentage of total employees, 1961	4.5%	6.4%	6.4%
2 Domestic tariff level, 1969	10.3%	15.6%	17.1%
3 U.S. tariff level, 1970	9.5%	10%	12.1%
4 Stage of fabrication	0.431	0.521	0.636
5 Four-firm concentration ratio	58.1	47.1	41.8

deficits, while technological intensity, as measured by the ratio of professional and technical workers to total employees, does not.

American tariff levels also appear related to relative trade deficits in an expected fashion. Import duties as a percentage of total imports in 1970 averaged 9.5 per cent for the first industry set, increasing to 10 per cent in the second set, and 12.1 per cent in the third.[18] Consistent with the studies by Baumann and Wilkinson, higher American tariffs are seen to be consistently related to trade deficits in Canadian industries.

Two other factors were related to our relative trade balance measure: a stage of fabrication index measured as the ratio of other final demand to total output, and the four-firm industrial concentration ratio.[19] On prior grounds, we would expect industries with higher fabrication indices to suffer relatively greater net trade deficits, since other studies have shown that favourable net trade balances are associated with industries largely manufacturing producer goods. The average value of the stage of fabrication index for industries in the first set is 0.431, increases to 0.521 in the second set, and to 0.636 in the third set. The four-firm

18 Calculated import duties for equivalent American industries are taken from U.S. Department of Commerce, 1974.

19 The stage of fabrication index was taken from Lermer, 1974, while the four firm concentration ratio is provided in Department of Consumer and Corporate Affairs, 1974.

concentration measure was used, as in Baumann's study, as a proxy for the different firm level economies such as economies in research and development, marketing, risk-bearing, and input purchasing. The four-firm concentration ratio for our industry sample decreases from an average value of 58.1 for the first set, to 47.1 for the second, and 41.8 for the third. The result with respect to the concentration variable is consistent with results obtained by Baumann for his preferred specification of Canadian trade patterns, that is, industry concentration was positively related to an industry's trade balance (Baumann, 1974*b*, Table 4). Carlsson, in a related study, found that efficiency levels in twenty-six Swedish manufacturing industries were positively related to the four-firm concentration ratio (Carlsson, 1972). The interpretation of the finding is that, for Canada, the concentration ratio reflects the existence of firm-level economies of scale; however, a factor that should be considered in interpreting the result is the significant influence that the motor vehicle industry has on the calculated concentration ratio for the first set.

In spite of the rather crude analysis, our results accord reasonably well with those of other studies. Industries for which Canada enjoys a relative trade surplus are characterized by lower domestic and American tariff levels, less processing for final use as a percentage of total output, and greater levels of concentration. The degree of comparative disadvantage across our industry sample is seen to be consistently related to Canada-United States tariff levels and stage of fabrication and inversely related to the ratio of industrial concentration, but is unrelated to the index of professional and technical workers. This finding suggests that the comparative disadvantage Canada suffers in technology-based industries does not reflect unique structural characteristics of these industries. Rather, internationally competitive performance in these industries is thwarted by the same sets of factors influencing production efficiency in other manufacturing industries, primarily short product lengths of run associated with domestic and American tariffs.

CONCLUSION

Considerations of the effects of North American tariffs on Canadian real income levels have generally focused on the static production and consumption costs associated with inefficiencies in production assuming existing technology. The regional implications of tariff-induced inefficiencies were discussed in Chapter 3 where it was concluded that an important long-term result of freer trade would be continued increases in real income levels of urban workers in Ontario and Quebec.

The thrust of this concluding section is to suggest that estimates of 'static' production inefficiencies understate the true costs associated with the North American tariff structure. While precise estimates are unobtainable, there is good reason, as well as evidence, to presume that dynamic inefficiencies associated with slower rates of technological change derive from tariff protection. The first round production effects of such costs would fall disproportionately on factors of production in the Ontario industrial sector. Ontario is a more manufacturing-intensive province than other regions of Canada; moreover, a higher percentage of Ontario's manufacturing output is concentrated in 'high-technology'[20] industries than is true elsewhere in the country. Specifically, total value added in manufacturing as a percentage of total value added for goods-producing industries in 1969 was approximately 78 per cent for Ontario and approximately 50 per cent for the rest of Canada. Total value added in fifteen 'high-technology' industries as a percentage total value added in manufacturing in 1971 was approximately 22 per cent in Ontario and approximately 17 per cent for the rest of the country.

The implication of the foregoing analysis is that science policy is complementary to broader commercial policies, including tariff policies. To the extent that trade liberalization would result in increased rates of industrial innovation and diffusion, Ontario has a particularly strong vested interest in such policies.

20 The following industries were classified as being 'high-technology' industries based upon the classification adopted by the Ministry of State for Science and Technology: petroleum and coal products; chemical and chemical products; man-made fibre; hardware, tool, and cutlery manufacturers; heating refrigeration, and air conditioning; agricultural implements; miscellaneous machinery and equipment; office machinery; aircraft and parts; railroad rolling stock; miscellaneous vehicle manufacturers; communications equipment; miscellaneous electrical products; pharmaceuticals and medicines; instruments and related products.

APPENDIX A

Additional tables

TABLE 1

Payments to Canadian industry for research and experimental development, 1966-67 to
1971-72 (millions of dollars)

Department or agency	1966-67	1967-68	1968-69	1969-70	1970-71	1971-72
AECB	–	–	–	–	0.1	0.1
AECL	28.5	27.2	35.8	33.3	30.6	22.1
Canadian Transport Commission	–	–	–	–	0.4	0.4
Communications	–	–	3.3	2.7	3.9	4.0
Energy, Mines and Resources	–	–	0.4	0.1	11.3	3.4
Environment	–	–	–	0.7	1.2	1.5
Fisheries and Forestry	0.8	0.3	0.1	–	–	–
ITC	25.8	31.3	45.7	52.1	67.0	82.6
National Defence	24.1	19.7	17.0	13.7	13.3	16.8
NRC	4.2	5.0	5.8	6.2	7.4	8.6
Public Works	–	–	–	0.1	0.1	0.1
Transport – Other	0.4	0.9	0.6	0.7	0.2	0.4
Other	0.1	0.1	0.2	0.1	0.1	0.1
TOTAL	83.9	84.5	108.9	109.7	135.6	140.1

SOURCE: Report of the Senate Special Committee on Science Policy, *A Science Policy for
Canada*, Vol. 2, 1972, p. 587

TABLE 2

Per cent distribution of national research and development by sector of performance and country, 1967

	Business enterprise	Government	Higher education	Private non-profit
Switzerland	76.5	6.3	17.1	–
Sweden	69.9	14.2	15.5	0.4
U.S.A.	69.8	14.5	12.2	3.6
Germany	68.2	5.1	16.3	10.4
Belgium	66.8	10.4	21.4	1.3
U.K.	64.9	24.8	7.8	2.5
Japan	62.5	13.0	22.9	1.6
Netherlands	58.1	2.7	17.7	21.5
France	54.2	32.1	12.9	0.8
Canada	37.7	35.6	26.7	

SOURCE: Report of The Senate Special Committee on Science Policy, *A Science Policy for Canada*, Vol. 1, 1970, p. 128

TABLE 3

Distribution of total national research and development expenditures by type of activity and country, 1967

Country	Development (%)	Applied research (%)	Fundamental research (%)
Switzerland	Not available	Not available	14.5
U.K.	64.6	24.4	11.0
U.S.A.	64.3	21.6	14.1
Netherlands	48.7	n.a.	n.a.
France	47.8	n.a.	n.a.
Japan	42.5	30.8	26.7
Canada	38.9	38.0	23.1
Belgium	37.2	42.2	20.5

SOURCE: Report of the Senate Special Committee on Science Policy, *A Science Policy for Canada*, Vol. I, 1970, p. 125

TABLE 4

Cost distribution breakdown for innovation activity

Activity	Percentage of Total Cost
Research – advanced	
Development – basic invention	5-10
Engineering and	
designing the product	10-20
Tooling – Manufacturing engineering	
(getting Ready for manufacture)	40-60
Manufacturing	
Start-up expenses	5-15
Marketing	
Start-up expenses	10-25

SOURCE: Report of the Senate Special Committee on Science Policy, *A Science Policy for Canada*, Vol. 2, 1972, p. 395

TABLE 5

Four performance indicators of technological innovation in ten industrially advanced countries

Country	Number industrial employees ['000]	I Location of 100 significant innovations since 1945			II Monetary receipts for patents etc., 1963-64			Percent Share of Ten Countries' Mfd. Exports	III Number of patents taken out in Foreign countries, 1963			IV Export performance in research-intensive product groups 1963-65			Composite Rank
		Absolute no.	With USA Base 100	Rank	Absolute $ million	With USA base 100	Rank		Absolute no. [000's]	With USA base 100	Rank	% share of 10 countries	With USA base 100	Rank	
Belgium	1,645	1	20.6	5	7.9	34.2	5	5.8	1.8	12.4	10	3.0	37.6	10	8
Canada	2,428	0	0	10	6.2	18.3	8	5.5	1.9	13.9	9	2.0	38.3	9	10
France	7,940	2	8.5	8	46.3	41.9	4	9.8	9.3	38.1	6	6.5	48.2	8	6
Germany	12,385	14	38.3	4	49.4	28.7	7	18.1	29.9	64.7	2	21.1	84.7	2	3 =
Italy	7,776	3	13.2	7	9.9	9.1	9	7.5	4.6	24.6	7	5.7	55.2	6	7
Japan	17,129	4	7.9	9	5.9	2.4	10	8.1	3.5	17.4	8	5.9	52.9	7	9
Netherlands	1,847	1	18.3	6	26.0	101.2	1	5.9	6.4	43.6	5	5.9	72.7	5	5
Sweden	1,535	4	88.4	2	7.1	33.3	6	3.5	3.8	43.7	4	4.0	83.1	3	3 =
U.K.	11,798	18	51.8	3	76.1	46.4	3	13.2	15.2	45.2	3	13.9	76.5	4	2
U.S.A.	25,063	74	100.0	1	386.7	100.0	2	22.6	56.3	100.0	1	31.1	100.0	1	1

NOTE: For indicators I and II, the ranking was derived by dividing the absolute values by the number of industrial employees to correct for country size. For indicators III and IV, the ranking was derived by dividing the absolute values by the percentage share of the ten countries' manufactured exports.

SOURCE: Report of The Senate Special Committee on Science Policy, *A Science Policy For Canada*, Vol. 1, 1970, p. 135

TABLE 6

Income relatives, science and all occupations (persons 15 years and over who worked in 1970)

Canada

1 $\dfrac{\text{Mean income for occupations in natural sciences, engineering and mathematics}}{\text{Mean income for all occupations}} = 1.6048$

2 $\dfrac{\text{Median income for occupations in sciences, engineering and mathematics}}{\text{Median income for all occupations}} = 1.7114$

Ontario

3 $\dfrac{\text{Mean income for occupations in sciences, engineering and mathematics}}{\text{Mean income for all occupations}} = 1.6228$

4 $\dfrac{\text{Median income for occupations in sciences, engineering and mathematics}}{\text{Median income for all occupations}} = 1.7173$

SOURCE: *Census of Canada, 1971* (Ottawa: Information Canada, 1974 and 1975), Vol. 1, pp. 14-1 and 2, Vol. 2, 17-71 and 72

TABLE 7

Relative supply and relative incomes of scientific workers: Canada versus U.S., 1970

Canada

1 $\dfrac{\text{Number of scientific workers}}{\text{Number of all employed persons}} = 0.0256$

2 $\dfrac{\text{Mean income of scientific workers}}{\text{Mean income of all employed persons}} = 1.6048$

U.S.

1 $\dfrac{\text{Number of scientific workers}}{\text{Number of all employed persons}} = 0.0297$

2 $\dfrac{\text{Mean income of scientific workers}}{\text{Mean income of all employed persons}} = 1.6820$

SOURCES: *Census of Canada, 1971*, and U.S. Department of Commerce, *1970 Census of Population*, Subject Report 7-C, *Occupation By Industry*, Table One and Subject Report 8-B, *Earnings By Occupation and Education*, Table One (Washington: U.S. Government Printing Office, 1973)

TABLE 8

Percentage of scientific and technical workers having five or more years of higher education (Canada and U.S., 1970)

Canada	U.S.
1 Engineers = 12	1 Engineers = 24
2 Life and physical scientists = 39	2 Life and physical scientists = 50

SOURCES: A. Atkinson, T. Barnes, and N. Richardson, *Canada's Highly Qualified Manpower Resources* (Ottawa: Department of Manpower and Immigration, 1970) and U.S. Department of Commerce, *1970 Census of Population*, Subject Report 8-B, *Earnings By Occupation and Education*, Table One

Sample industries

SIC code	Industry
1094	Wineries
151	Leaf tobacco processors
153	Tobacco products manufacturers
162	Rubber products
165	Plastics fabricating industries, NES
172	Leather tanneries
174	Shoe factories
175	Leather glove factories
181	Cotton yarn and cloth mills
182	Wool yarn and cloth mills
183	Man-made fibre yarn and cloth mills
231	Hosiery mills
248	Foundation garment industry
252	Veneer and plywood mills
2541	Sash door and other millwork plants
256	Wooden box factories
2619	Household furniture mfs., NES
264	Office furniture mfs.
266	Miscellaneous furniture and equipment mfs.
268	Electric lamp and shade mfs.
272	Asphalt roofing manufacturers
291	Iron and steel mills
292	Steel pipe and tube mills
294	Iron foundries
301	Boiler and plateworks
3039	Ornamental and architectural metal, NES
304	Metal stamping, pressing, and coating

SIC code	Industry
305	Wire and wire products
306	Hardware tool and cutlery mfs.
307	Heating equipment mfs.
311	Agricultural implements
316	Commercial refrigeration and air-conditioning equipment
321	Aircraft and aircraft parts mfs.
323	Motor vehicle mfs.
324	Truck body and trailer mfs.
325	Motor vehicle parts and accessories mfs.
326	Railroad rolling stock
327	Shipbuilding and repair
331	Mfs. of small electrical appliances
332	Mfs. of major appliances
334	Mfs. of household radio and TV receivers
335	Communications equipment
336	Mfs. of electrical industrial equipment
338	Mfs. of wire and cable
3391	Battery mfs.
3651	Petroleum refining
373	Mfs. of plastics and synthetic resins
374	Mfs. of pharaceuticals and medicines
375	Paint and varnish mfs.
376	Mfs. of soaps and cleaning compounds
377	Mfs. of toilet preparations
378	Mfs. of industrial chemicals
393	Sporting goods and toys
3991	Broom, brush, and mop mfs.

Bibliography

Alchian, A. (1959) 'Costs and outputs.' In M. Abramovitz et al., *The Allocation of Economic Resources: Essays in Honour of B.F. Haley* (Stanford: Stanford University Press)

Australian Government Publishing Service. (1972) *A Study of the Rate of Diffusion of New Technology within Australian Industry* (Canberra)

Axline, W. Andrew, et al. (1974) *Continental Community? Independence and Integration in North America* (Toronto: McClelland and Stewart)

Bain, Joe S. (1966) *International Differences in Industrial Structure: Eight Nations in the 1950's* (New Haven: Yale University Press)

Balassa, Bela. (1965) 'Trade liberalisation and revealed comparative advantage.' The Manchester School of Economics and Social Studies

Baldwin, Robert and Mutti, John H. (1973) 'Policy issues in Adjustment assistance: the United States.' In Helen Hughes, ed., *Prospects for Partnership: Industrialization and Trade Policies in the 1970's* (Baltimore: Johns Hopkins Press)

Barber, Clarence L. (1955) 'Canadian tariff policy.' *Canadian Journal of Economics and Political Science,* 513-30

Barrows, D. (1973) 'Canadian Exports and Imports 1968-70.' Mimeo. (Toronto: Peat, Marwick and Partners)

Baumann, H.G. (1974a) 'The rationalizing of Canadian Industry: a comment.' *Canadian Journal of Economics* 7, 311-16

– (1974b) 'Structural characteristics of Canada's pattern of trade.' University of Western Ontario, Research Report 4701, Mimeo. (Vancouver: University of British Columbia)

Beigie, Carl E. (1970) *The Canada-U.S. Automotive Agreement: An Evaluation* (Montreal: Canadian-American Committee)
- (1972) 'The Canada-U.S. auto pact.' In J. Chant, ed., *Canadian Perspectives in Economics* (Toronto: Collier-Macmillan) Chapter D2.
Berglas, Eitan and Razin, Assaf. (1974) 'Protection and real profits.' *Canadian Journal of Economics* 7, 655-64
Bergman, Joel (1974) 'Commercial policy, allocative efficiency and X-efficiency.' *Quarterly Journal of Economics*, 409-33
Bertram, Gordon W. (1965) *The Contribution of Education to Economic Growth*. Staff Study No. 12 for the Economic Council of Canada (Ottawa: Queen's Printer)
Black, Naomi. (1974) 'Absorptive systems are impossible: The Canadian-American relationship as a disparate dyad.' In W. Andrew Axline et al., *Continental Community? Independence and Integration in North America* (Toronto: McClelland and Stewart)
Bloch, Harry. (1974) 'Prices, costs and profits in Canadian manufacturing: the influence of tariffs and concentration.' *Canadian Journal of Economics* 7, 594-610
Bourgault, Pierre. (1973) *Innovation and the Structure of Canadian Industry*. Science Council of Canada, Special Study Number 23 (Ottawa: Information Canada)
Brash, Donald T. (1966) *American Investment in Australian Industry* (Cambridge: Harvard University Press)
Breton, Albert. (1964) 'The economics of nationalism.' *Journal of Political Economy* 72, 376-86
- (1972) 'The economic approach to nationalism.' In J. Chant, ed., *Canadian Perspectives in Economics* (Toronto: Collier-Macmillan)
- (1974) *A Conceptual Basis for an Industrial Strategy*. Economic Council of Canada (Ottawa: Information Canada)
Campbell, Duncan A.E. (1971) 'Forms of executive and senior management compensation in the U.S. and Canada.' Mimeo. (Toronto)
Canada Year Book. (1973) (Ottawa: Statistics Canada)
Canadian-American Committee. (1965) *A Possible Plan for a Canada-U.S. Free Trade Area* (Montreal: Private Planning Association of Canada)
Carlsson, Bo. (1972) 'The measurement of efficiency in production: an application to Swedish manufacturing industries, 1968' *Swedish Journal of Economics*, 468-85
Caves, Richard E. and Associates (1968) *Britain's Economic Prospects* (Washington: The Brookings Institution)
Caves, Richard E. (1975) *Diversification, Foreign Investment and Scale in North American Manufacturing Industries*. Economic Council of Canada (Ottawa: Information Canada)

Clement, Wallace. (1975) *The Canadian Corporate Elite: An Analysis of Economic Power* (Toronto: McClelland and Stewart)

Cook, Ramsay. (1971) *The Maple Leaf Forever: Essays on Nationalism and Politics in Canada* (Toronto: Macmillan)

Crookell, Harold. (1973) The transmission of technology across national boundaries.' *The Business Quarterly*, Autumn, 52-61

Crookell, Harold and Wrigley, Leonard. (1975) 'Canadian response to multi-national enterprise.' *The Business Quarterly*, Spring, 58-68

Dales, John. (1966) *The Protective Tariff in Canada's Development* (Toronto: University of Toronto Press)

Daly, D.J. (1966) 'The scope for monetary policy – a synthesis.' *Conference on Stabilization Policies*. Economic Council of Canada (Ottawa: Queen's Printer)

- (1968) 'Why growth rates differ: a summary and appraisal.' *Review of Income and Wealth* 14, 75-93

- (1969) 'Business cycles in Canada: their postwar persistence.' In Martin Bronfenbrenner, ed., *Is the Business Cycle Obsolete?* (New York: John Wiley and Sons, pp. 45-65)

- (1970) *A Submission by the International Nickel Company of Canada Limited, on the Proposals for Tax Reform* (Toronto: International Nickel Company of Canada Limited, Appendix D1)

- (1972*a*) 'Uses of International price and output data.' In D.J. Daly, ed., *International Comparisons of Prices and Output* (New York: Columbia University Press, pp. 85-141)

- (1972*b*) 'Combining inputs to secure a measure of total factor input.' *Review of Income and Wealth* 18, 27-53

- (1972*c*) 'Fiscal policy – an assessment.' In J. Chant, ed., *Canadian Perspectives in Economics* (Toronto: Collier-Macmillan)

- (1973) 'Trading giants and Canadian options.' In Heinz J. Neunteufel, ed., *The Future of American Corporations in the European Economic Community* (Schenectady, N.Y.: Union College) pp. 501-25.

- (1974) 'New approaches in the development of managers' and 'Managerial manpower in Canada.' In H.C. Jain, ed., *Contemporary Issues in Canadian Personnel Administration* (Toronto: Prentice-Hall)

- (1974) 'Managerial manpower in Canada.' In H.C. Jain, ed., *Contemporary Issues in Canadian Personnel Administration* (Toronto: Prentice-Hall) pp. 98-105

Daly, D.J. and Walters, D. (1967) 'Factors in Canada-United States real income differences.' *Review of Income and Wealth* 13, 285-309

Daly, D.J., Keys, B.A., and Spence, E.J. (1968) *Scale and Specialization in Canadian Manufacturing*. Staff Study No. 21 for the Economic Council of Canada (Ottawa: Queen's Printer)

Daly, D.J. and Peterson, Rein. (1973) 'On bridging the gaps.' *Management Science* 20, No. 4, 550-69

Daly, William G. (1972) 'The mobility of top business executives in Canada.' (MBA thesis, University of British Columbia), p. 68

Dauphin, Roma and Audet, Gerald. (1974) *The Regional Impact of Freer Trade in Canada*. Mimeo. (Ottawa: Economic Council of Canada)

Denison, Edward F. (1962) *The Sources of Economic Growth in the United States and the Alternatives Before Us* (New York: Committee for Economic Development)

- (1974) *Accounting for United States Economic Growth, 1929-1969* (Washington: The Brookings Institution)

- assisted by Poullier, Jean-Pierre. (1967) *Why Growth Rates Differ: Postwar Experience in Nine Western Countries* (Washington: The Brookings Institution)

Department of Consumer and Corporate Affairs. (1974) *Concentration in the Manufacturing Industries* (Ottawa: Information Canada)

Department of Industry, Trade and Commerce. (1970*a*) *Industrial Design Assistance Program* (Ottawa: Information Canada)

- (1970*b*) *Industrial Research and Development Incentives Act* (Ottawa: Information Canada)

- (1970*c*) *Program for the Advancement of Industrial Technology* (Ottawa: Information Canada)

- (1970*d*) Program to Enhance Productivity (Ottawa: Information Canada)

DIVO Institute for Economic Research, Social Research and Applied Mathematics. (1969) *American Subsidiaries in the Federal Republic of Germany* (Munich)

Downs, Anthony. (1957) *An Economic Theory of Democracy* (New York: Harper)

Dunning, John H. (1962) *American Investment in British Manufacturing Industry* (London: Oxford University Press)

Eastman, H.C. and Stykolt, S. (1967) *The Tariff and Competition in Canada* (Toronto: Macmillan)

Economic Council of Canada. (1968) *Fifth Annual Review* (Ottawa: Information Canada)

- (1969) *Interim Report on Competition Policy* (Ottawa: Queen's Printer)

- (1975) *Looking Outward, A New Trade Strategy for Canada* (Ottawa: Information Canada)

English, Edward, Wilkinson, Bruce W., and Eastman, H. (1972) *Canada and A Wider Economic Community* (Toronto: University of Toronto Press)

Enos, John L. (1962) 'Invention and innovation in the petroleum refining industry.' In *The Rate and Direction of Inventive Activity*. National Bureau of

Economic Research (Princeton: Princeton University Press)

Farmer, Richard N. and Richman, Barry M. (1971) *International Business*, 2nd ed. (Bloomington: Cedarwood)

– (1972) *Benevolent Aggression: The Necessary Impact of the Advanced Nations on Indigenous Peoples* (New York: McKay)

Fayerweather, John. (1973) *Foreign Investment in Canada: Prospects for National Policy* (White Plains: International Arts and Sciences Press)

Firestone, O.J. (1971) *The Economic Implication of Patents* (Ottawa: University of Ottawa Press)

Freeman, Richard B. (1971) *The Market for College-Trained Manpower* (Cambridge: Harvard University Press)

– (1975) 'Supply and salary adjustments to the changing science manpower market: physics, 1948-1973.' *American Economic Review* 65, 27-39

Fullerton, D.H. and Hampson, H.A. (1957) *Canadian Secondary Manufacturing Industry* (Ottawa: Queen's Printer)

Gebhardt, A. and Hertzold, O. (1974) 'Numerically controlled machine tools.' In R. Nasbeth and G.F. Ray, eds., *The Diffusion of Industrial Processes* (Cambridge: Cambridge University Press)

Geiger, Theodore. (1973) 'Toward a world of trading blocs?' In Donald S. Henley, ed., *International Business – 1973: A Selection of Current Readings* (East Lansing, Mich.: MSU International Business and Economic Studies)

Globerman, S. (1972) 'The empirical relationship between R & D and industrial growth in Canada.' *Applied Economics*, September, 181-95

– (1973) 'Market structure and R & D in Canadian manufacturing industries.' *The Quarterly Review of Economics and Business*, Summer, 59-67

– (1975a) 'Technological diffusion in the Canadian carpet industry.' *Research Policy*, Spring, 190-206

– (1975b) 'Technological diffusion in the Canadian tool and die industry' *The Review of Economics and Statistics* 57, No. 4, November, 428-34

– 'New technology adoption in the Canadian paper industry.' *Industrial Organization Review*, in press

Gordon, Walter. (1966) *A Choice for Canada: Independence or Colonial Status* (Toronto: McClelland and Stewart)

Gray Report, Government of Canada. (1972) *Foreign Direct Investment in Canada* (Ottawa: Information Canada)

Grey, Rodney de C. (1973) *The Development of the Canadian Anti-Dumpting System* (Montreal: Canadian Economic Policy Committee)

Grizzardi, Walter., Jr. (1966) *The Young Executives: How and Why Successful Managers Get Ahead* (New York: Mentor Executive Library)

Grubel, Herbert G. and Lloyd, P.J. (1975) *Intra-Industry Trade: The Theory and Measurement of International Trade in Differentiated Products*

(New York: John Wiley & Sons)

Gruber, W., Mehta, D., and Vernon, R. (1967) 'The R & D factor in international trade and international investment of United States industries.' *Journal of Political Economy* 75, 20-37

Haldi, John and Whitcomb, David. (1967) 'Economies of scale in industrial plants.' *Journal of Political Economy* 75, 373-85

Harberger, A. (1959) 'The fundamentals of economic progress in underdeveloped countries: using the resources at hand more effectively.' *American Economic Review* 49, 134-47

Haviland, W., Takacsy, N., and Cape, E. (1968) *Trade Liberalization and the Canadian Pulp and Paper Industry* (Toronto: University of Toronto Press)

Hirsch, S. (1956) 'The United States electronics industry in international trade.' *National Institute Economic Review* 34, 92-7

Hirshleifer, Jack. (1962) 'The firm's cost function: a successful reconstruction?' *Journal of Business*, July, 235-55

Hufbauer, G.C. (1966) *Synthetic Materials and the Theory of International Trade* Cambridge: Harvard University Press)

Hymer, Stephen H. and Resnick, Stephen A. (1971) 'International trade and uneven development.' In Jagdish N. Bhagwati et al., eds., *Trade, Balance of Payments and Growth* (Amsterdam: North-Holland) pp. 473-94.

– (1972) 'The multinational corporation and the problem of uneven development.' In *Economics and World Order* (New York: Macmillan)

Issues in Management Education. (1963) (Paris: OECD)

Janssen, L.H. (1961) *Free Trade, Protection and Customs Union* (Leiden: H.E. Stenfert Kroese)

Jenkins, Glenn P. (1972) 'Analysis of rates of returns from capital in Canada.' (Chicago: University of Chicago, Ph D Dissertation)

Johnson, Harry G. (1958) 'The gains from freer trade with Europe: an estimate.' Manchester School Economic and Social Studies 26, September, 247-55

– (1960) 'The cost of protection and the scientific tariff.' *Journal of Political Economy* 68, no. 4, August, 327-45

– (1965) 'A theoretical model of economic nationalism in new and developing states.' *Political Science Quarterly* 80, 169-85

– (1967) *Economic Nationalism in Old and New States* (© 1967 by The University of Chicago. All rights reserved. By permission of the author and the publisher)

Jordan, William A. (1972) 'Producer protection, prior market structure and the effects of government regulation.' *Journal of Law and Economics*, April, 151-76

Kelly, Frank. (1971) *Prospects for Scientists and Engineers in Canada* (Ottawa: Information Canada)

Knox, F.A., Barber, C.L., and Slater, D.W. (1955) *The Canadian Electrical*

Manufacturing Industry (Toronto: Canadian Electrical Manufacturers' Association)

Labour Canada. (1974) *Canadian Labour Income Recent Trends – The Current Picture* (Ottawa: Information Canada)

Legislative Assembly of Ontario. (1972) *Preliminary Report of the Select Committee on Economic and Cultural Nationalism* (Toronto: Queen's Printer)

Leibenstein, H. (1966) 'Allocative efficiency vs. 'X-efficiency'.' *American Economic Review* 56, 392-415

Leonard, W.N. (1971) 'Research and development in industrial growth.' *Journal of Political Economy* 79, 232-57

Lermer, George. (1973) 'Evidence from trade data regarding the rationalizing of Canadian industry.' *Canadian Journal of Economics* 6, 248-56

– (1974) 'Growth industries and tariff policy,' paper presented at the annual meeting of the Canadian Economic Association, June.

Levitt, Kari. (1970) *Silent Surrender: The Multinational Corporation in Canada* (Toronto: Macmillan)

Lyon, Peyton V. (1975) *Canada-United States Free Trade and Canadian Independence.* Economic Council of Canada (Ottawa: Information Canada)

Mackintosh, W.A. (1940) *The Economic Background of Dominion-Provincial Relations* (Ottawa: Queen's Printer)

Mansfield, Edwin. (1968*a*) *The Economics of Technological Change* (New York: W.W. Norton and Company)

– (1968*b*) 'The diffusion of a major manufacturing innovation.' In Mansfield et al., *Research and Innovation in the Modern Corporation* (New York: W.W. Norton and Company)

Marshall, Alfred. (1920) *Principles of Economics*, 8th ed. (London: Macmillan), p. 385

Maslove, Allan M. (1973) *The Pattern of Taxation in Canada* (Ottawa: Information Canada for the Economic Council of Canada)

Matthews, Roy A. (1971) *Industrial Viability in a Free Trade Economy: A Program of Adjustment Policies for Canada.* The Private Planning Association of Canada (Toronto: University of Toronto Press)

Mayer, Wolfgang. (1974) 'Short-run and long-run equilibrium for a small open economy.' *Journal of Political Economy* 82, 955-68

McDiarmid, O.J. (1946) *Commercial Policy in the Canadian Economy* (Cambridge: Harvard University Press

Melman, Seymour. (1975) 'Twelve propositions on productivity and the war economy.' *Challenge* 18, March/April, 7-11

Meyboom, P. (1970) *Technological Innovation in Canada.* Working Paper 7100 (Ottawa: Department of Finance)

Moore, Milton. (1970) *How Much Price Competition? The prerequisites of an effective Canadian competition policy* (Montreal: McGill-Queen's University Press)

Murray, J. Alex and Le Duc, Lawrence. (1975) *A Cross-Sectional Analysis of Canadian Public Attitudes Toward U.S. Equity Investment in Canada.* Working Paper 2 (Toronto: OEC)

Mussa, Michael. (1974) 'Tariffs and the distribution of income: the importance of factor specificity, substitutability, and intensity in the short and long run.' *Journal of Political Economy* 82, 1191-204

O'Connell, John F. (1972) 'The labor market for engineers: an alternative methodology.' *Journal of Human Resources*, Winter, 71-86

OECD (1963) *Issues in Management Education* (Paris: Organization for Economic Cooperation and Development)

Oi, Walter Y. (1962) 'Labor as a quasi-fixed factor.' *Journal of Political Economy* 70, 538-55

Okun, Arthur M. (1975) *Equality and Efficiency: The Big Tradeoff* (Washington: The Brookings Institution)

Pestieau, Caroline and Henry, Jacques. (1972) *Non-Tariff Trade Barriers as a Problem in International Development* (Montreal: Economic Policy Committee)

Porter, John. (1965) *The Vertical Mosaic: An Analysis of Social Class and Power in Canada* (Toronto: University of Toronto Press)

Posner, M.V. (1961) 'International trade and technical change.' *Oxford Economic Papers* 13, 323-41

Presthus, Robert. (1973) *Elite Accommodation in Canadian Politics* (Toronto: Macmillan)

Prices Division. (1967) 'Comparative consumer price levels in the United States and Canada.' Mimeo. (Ottawa: Dominion Bureau of Statistics)

Provincial Bank of Canada (1972) *Economic Review*, July/August, 1-6

Ray, G.F. (1969) 'The diffusion of new technology: a study of ten processes in nine industries.' *National Institute Economic Review*, 40-83

Report of the Senate Special Committee on Science Policy. (1970) *A Science Policy for Canada*, Vol. I (Ottawa: Information Canada)

Reynolds, W.A. (1968) *Innovation in the United States Carpet Industry 1947-1963* (New York: D. Van Nostrand Company, Inc.)

Richman, Barry M. and Copen, Melvyn. (1972) *International Management and Economic Development* (New York: McGraw-Hill)

Romeo, A. (1975) 'Interindustry and interfirm differences in the rate of diffusion of an innovation.' *Review of Economics and Statistics* 57, no. 3 August

Rosenbluth, Gideon. (1957) *Concentration in Canadian Manufacturing*

Industries. National Bureau of Economic Research (Princeton: Princeton University Press)

Rotstein, Abraham. (1973) *The Precarious Homestead: Essays on Economics, Technology and Nationalism* (Toronto: New Press)

Rotstein, Abraham and Lax, Gary, eds. (1974) *Getting it Back: A Program for Canadian Independence*. The Committee for an Independent Canada (Toronto: Clarke-Irwin)

Russell, Peter, ed. (1966) *Nationalism in Canada* (Toronto: McGraw-Hill)

Safarian, A.E. (1966) *Foreign Ownership of Canadian Industry* (Toronto: McGraw-Hill)

– (1969) *The Performance of Foreign-Owned Firms in Canada*. The Canadian-American Committee (Montreal: Private Planning Association of Canada)

Salter, W.E.G. (1966) *Productivity and Technical Changes* (Cambridge: Cambridge University Press)

Sargent, J.R. (1973) 'The distribution of scientific manpower.' In B.R. Williams, ed., *Science and Technology in Economic Growth* (New York: John Wiley and Sons)

Scherer, F.M. (1973) 'The determinants of industrial plant sizes in six nations.' *Review of Economics and Statistics* 55, 135-45

– (1974) 'Trans-national mergers as a source of production scale economies.' Presented at Tokyo Conference on International Economy and Competition Policy. Mimeo (Berlin: International Institute of Management)

– (1975) *The Economics of Multi-Plant Operation: An International Comparisons Analysis* (Cambridge: Harvard University Press)

Science Council of Canada. (1971) *Innovation in a Cold Climate*, Report Number 15, October (Ottawa: Information Canada)

Scitovsky, J. (1958) *Economic Theory and Western European Integration* (Stanford: Stanford University Press)

Shearer, Ronald A., Young, John H., and Munro, Gordon R. (1973) *Trade Liberalization and a Regional Economy: Studies of the Impact of Free Trade on British Columbia* (Toronto: University of Toronto Press)

Statistics Canada. (1974) *Aggregate Productivity Measures, 1946-1972* (Ottawa: Information Canada)

– (1974) *Canadian Statistical Review* (Ottawa: Information Canada)

Stegemann, Klaus. (1974) *Canadian Non-Tariff Barriers to Trade* (Montreal: Canadian Economic Policy Committee)

Stigler, George. (1971) 'The theory of economic regulation.' *Bell Journal of Economics and Management Science*, Spring, 3-21

Stockfish, J.A. (1969) *Measuring the Opportunity Cost of Government Investment* (Arlington, Virginia: Institute for Defence Analysis)

Stolper, Wolfgang F. and Samuelson, Paul A. (1941) 'Protection and real wages.'
  Review of Economic Studies 9, 58-73
Tilton, John. (1971) *International Diffusion of Technology: The Case of Semi-
  Conductors* (Washington: The Brookings Institution)
U.S. Department of Commerce. (1967) *Technological Innovation* (Washington:
  Government Printing Office)
- (1973a) *1970 Census of Population*, Vol. 1 (Washington: Government
  Printing Office)
- (1973b) *Survey of Current Business*, April (Washington: Government Printing
  Office)
- (1974) *U.S. Commodity Exports and Imports as Related to Output, 1970
  and 1971* (Washington: Government Printing Office)
Utterback, J.M. (1974) 'Innovation in industry and the diffusion of technology.'
  Science, February, 620-6
Vernon, Raymond. (1966) 'International investment and international trade in
  the product cycle.' *Quarterly Journal of Economics* 85, 190-207
- ed., (1970) *The Technology Factor in International Trade* (New York:
  Columbia University Press)
Von Zur-Muehlen, Max. (1971) *Business Education and Faculty at Canadian
  Universities*. The Economic Council of Canada (Ottawa: Information Canada)
Wahn Report. (1970) *The Eleventh Report of the Standing Committee on
  External Affairs and National Defence Respecting Canada-U.S. Relations*
  (Ottawa: Queen's Printer)
Waisglass, Harry J. (1974) *Compensation in Canada*. Notes for an address to the
  Conference Board of Canada (Ottawa: Canada Department of Labour)
Walters, Dorothy. (1968) *Canadian Income Levels and Growth: An International
  Perspective*. Staff Study No. 23 for the Economic Council of Canada (Ottawa:
  Queen's Printer)
- (1970) *Canadian Growth Revisited, 1950-1967).* Staff Study No. 28 for the
  Economic Council of Canada (Ottawa: Information Canada)
Warner, W. Lloyd and Abegglen, James C. (1955) *Occupational Mobility in
  American Business and Industry, 1929-1952* (Minneapolis: University of
  Minnesota Press)
Watkins, Melville H. (1972) 'The Canadian quandary.' In J.L. Granatstein and
  Peter Stevens, eds., *Forum, Canadian Life and Letters, 1920-1970* (Toronto:
  University of Toronto Press) pp. 371-3
Watkins Report. (1968) *Foreign Ownership and the Structure of Canadian
  Industry* (Ottawa: Queen's Printer)
Weiser, L. and Jay, K. (1972) 'Determinants of the commodity structure of U.S.

Trade: comment.' *American Economic Review*, June, 459-64

Wells, Louis J., Jr., ed. (1972) *The Product Life Cycle and International Trade* (Boston: Harvard Business School, Division of Research)

Wernelsfelder, J. (1960) 'The short-term effect of lowering import duties in Germany.' *Economic Journal* 70, 94-104

West, E.C. (1971) *Canada-United States Price and Productivity Differences in Manufacturing Industries, 1963.* Staff Study No. 32 for the Economic Council of Canada (Ottawa: Information Canada)

Wilkinson, Bruce W. (1966) *Studies in the Economics of Education.* Economics and Research Branch, Department of Labour, Occasional Paper No. 4 (Ottawa: Queen's Printer)

– (1968) *Canada's International Trade: An Analysis of Recent Trends and Patterns* (Montreal: Private Planning Association of Canada)

Williams, James R. (1973) *The Canadian-U.S. Tariff and Canadian Industry.* Mimeo. (Hamilton: Department of Economics, McMaster University)

Wilson, Andrew H. (1968) *Science, Technology and Innovation.* Special Study Number 8 for the Economic Council of Canada (Ottawa: Queen's Printer)

Winston, Gordon C. (1974) 'The theory of capacity utilization and idleness.' *Journal of Economic Literature* 12, 4, 1301-20

Wonnacott, Paul and Wonnacott, Ronald J. (1968) *U.S.-Canadian Free Trade: The Potential Impact on the Canadian Economy* (Montreal: Private Planning Association of Canada)

Wonnacott, Ronald J. (1975) *Canada's Trade Options.* Economic Council of Canada (Ottawa: Information Canada)

Wonnacott, Ronald J. and Wonnacott, Paul. (1967) *Free Trade Between the United States and Canada, The Potential Economic Effects* (Cambridge: Harvard University Press. ©1967 by the President and Fellows of Harvard College. By permission of the author and the publisher)

Young, J.H. (1957) *Canadian Commercial Policy* (Ottawa: Queen's Printer)

Ontario Economic Council Research Studies

Lightning Source UK Ltd.
Milton Keynes UK
UKHW012359200722
406167UK00001B/286